Satisfied Woman

*"Discovering True Worth, Peace,
Fulfillment & Abundant Living"*

Sarah Ann Goebel

xulon
PRESS

Dedications

First, I dedicate this book to my mother, Marcia Hall, who went home to be with the Lord on September 30, 2006. Thank you, mom, for imparting to me perseverance and commitment. I love you and although you have gone home to our Lord, you continue to live here within my heart.

Second, I dedicate this book to my two children who were born of my flesh. Ginger, I am so proud of the caring and faithful woman you have become. Jason, I am equally as proud of the responsible and caring man you are today. Thank you for your love and thank you for being my friend. You both are special gifts from God to my life. I thank God for you and I praise Him that you are also my sister and brother in Christ.

Third, I dedicate this book to the beautiful ladies whom God has allowed me the opportunity to pour into and mentor at some level in your lives. Thank you for allowing me into your lives and thank you for enriching mine so.

Fourth, I dedicate this book to all women who persevere the necessary process in order to see change, and endure the journey to receive the prize that lies at the end of it where you will be able to say I AM A SATISFIED WOMAN!

May you always live your lives by faith;

be fulfilled and satisfied;

and may your lives glorify God the Father

and the Lord Jesus Christ!

Appreciation

Thank you, Tara Sinclair, for your patience & willingness to read through the roughest rough draft manuscript for this book. Your comments gave me some much needed direction in the early stages of writing. Thank you for being a sister in Christ who encourages and supports. Thank you for all you do for us and our Manna family. I thank God for you always.

Thank you, Gloria Cotten for your sisterhood, encouragement and professional excellence in editing this project. Thank you for your example, for believing in me and the work God has called me to and for the opportunity you have given me to walk out in and grow in that calling. You have positively impacted me beyond words. I thank God exceedingly for sending you into my life as a mentor and friend and I love you dearly.

I give thanks to my patient, unselfish and loyal husband Jon, who always loves me and encourages me in all that the Lord sets before me. Thank you, Jon, for not allowing me to quit on the dreams that God places in my heart and thank you for being my pastor, husband, lover and friend. When God brought you into my life, He redeemed and restored all that had been lost and broken. Thank you for the overflow of joy and satisfaction that is in my life because of you.

I thank Laryssa Toomer, who encouraged me to begin writing and speaking and who unselfishly shared her resources and knowledge to launch me on this journey of "writing and proclaiming His Answer". I will always remember the laughter and the tears we shared during our season of close friendship. You are, indeed, a special lady and valued friend to all who have the privilege to get close to you.

I thank Michael Fletcher, as spiritual mentor and oversight to my husband and myself. Michael, your faithfulness to God and your leadership to your church and the churches of GCI as President of Grace Churches International is a blessing to so many of us. Thank you for giving us a strong biblical foundation to *build our lives upon* and to share with others from. Thank you for believing in us and that which God called us to.

I thank the Board Members for Declaring His Answer Ministries. Thank you for your friendship and sisterhood in the Lord; thank you for all your prayers, encouragement and service and for believing in the vision for this book and the ministry God has given me. I am so blessed to know each of you and honored to co-labor with you in advancing the Kingdom of God.

I thank my girlfriends, Lyvonne Snyder and Cheryl Ertel. Thank you for your prayers and for holding me up when I have grown weary. Thank you for your commitment to our friendship relationship. Your loyalty and faithfulness will not go unnoticed by our Father. I love ya'll lots!

I thank you Russ, Craig and Dale for your faithful friendship to my husband and for including in your weekly prayers, prayers for me and the completion of this book.

Thank you to the Manna Church family who have remembered me in their prayers and encouraged me to continue "declaring His Answer" as the Lord guides.

I thank my daughter Ginger, and my son Jason, who are God's precious gifts to my life. Thank you for believing in me. I, too, believe in you! I thank God for allowing me to have the privilege of bringing you into this world to be your mother; and I thank God for His love in your life making up for the places and times I fell short. I am so proud of both of you and I pray for your relationship with the Lord to continue to grow in intimacy while He brings you to a place of fulfillment and satisfaction.

Thank you my parents, Jim and Marcia Hall who brought me into the world and have always been there for me. If I could have picked out any couple in the world for parents, I would have chosen you.

Your love shown in your many sacrifices made for my brothers and I as well as your grandchildren is to be praised. Thank you Dad for taking care of mom! I love you!

And above all, I thank my Lord Jesus Christ for loving me, saving me, enabling me, comforting and encouraging me to bring me "to such a time as this." Thank you Lord for allowing me to be a part of what you are doing on the earth. To You, Lord Jesus, be the glory and honor forever!

Table of Contents

INTRODUCTION

J esus said, "The thief comes only in order to steal and kill and destroy. *I came that they may have and enjoy life, and have it in abundance (to the full, till it overflows)"* (John 10:10 AMP). I ask you – Are you enjoying your life? Are you enjoying it in abundance? What would a joy-filled, satisfied, abundant life look like to you?

Perhaps you picture a new home, a new car, a new man, any man! Perhaps it is a closet full of Liz Claiborne clothes with shoes, purses and accessories to match. Perhaps it is that job promotion or change of jobs. Have you ever really wanted something or someone so desperately that you just knew your life would always be empty and meaningless without it?

Have you ever had the thrill of actually *receiving* that which you yearned for so desperately only to discover that after a few months of having it, the blessing had worn off and you were asking yourself, "Why did I think I could not live without this?"

As I shepherd women, I hear this story frequently —"I can't get no satisfaction. I try and I try…" but I can't seem to get it. Okay, I realize I have revealed I have not always been a Christian and I am dating myself as well. As some of you know, "(I Can't Get No) Satisfaction" is a title of a secular hit song by the Rolling Stones released in the 60's. But truly, the desire for satisfaction seems greater today than ever before, and it is sought for as much in the *Christian* world as it is in the *secular* world. I have witnessed myself along with many other people, rich and poor, young and old, Christians and non-Christians, all searching for what seems to be a nonexistent state of contentment. There is dissatisfaction with our jobs, ministries, health, finances, and circumstances, people who are in our lives, material goods, our selves and God. What is the problem?

The problem is that in our culture we are *not* trained to be *content*. On the other hand, we *are* trained to be *discontent*. Just look at the advertisements on TV, in magazines, everywhere. There is a continuous bombardment of enticements – things and ideas designed to entangle us and prevent us from living a satisfied and abundant life. All around us we are being *taught* to believe in an accumulation of things for our satisfaction. A desire for that which we do not have, whatever it might be, is constantly being cultivated. Yet, satisfaction is not found.

As people depend on circumstances, people and things to bring them contentment, they *do* experience a measure of happiness – a kind of emotional uplifting. They soon discover, however, that anything which brings an emotional high can also bring an emotional low with the event of change; therefore, their satisfaction in life varies from year to year; month to month; week to week; day to day and even minute to minute. The end result is dissatisfaction.

Satisfaction — is it nonexistent, or could it be that we are looking for this valuable non-tangible in all the wrong places and in all the wrong ways? Can one truly discover and experience a life of true satisfaction? If so, where do we go to find it? How do we get it? If we get it, how do we keep it?

I ask you – What is your heart's desire? Could it be that while you have been in search of it, you have missed the enjoyment, satisfaction and purpose God had for you *yesterday?* How about *today?* Are you frantically running from one thing to another, from one person to another, from one job to another? Are you shopping for some *thing,* some *one* or some *circumstance* to bring satisfaction to your life?

I believe that most if not all of us, have experienced this cycle of wanting and receiving to only discover we still want more, more times than we would like to admit. Some of you find yourselves on a continuous merry-go-round on a non-ending pursuit for more of some thing or some one, for a sense of value, peace, and contentment but it is nowhere to be found. Some of you have a restlessness inside of you that just won't quit!

There is hope and satisfaction is available. I have to tell you though that personal satisfaction does not come *easily* and it does not come *naturally*. So where do we find it and how do we get it?

Hope is found in the Bible. Paul tells us in Philippians 4:11 that he learned to be content no matter what his circumstances were. Notice Paul uses the word *learned*. Paul learned the true secret to life and he wanted to share it with the Philippians. If Paul learned it, you and I can too.

John 10:10 tells us that Jesus came that we might have life and have it more abundantly. What is it He is telling us? According to Strong's, the Greek word for abundantly is *"Perissos"* and means superabundance, excessive, overflowing, surplus, over and above, more than enough, profuse, extraordinary, above the ordinary, more than sufficient.[1] He is saying He came that we could experience an extraordinary life—one above the ordinary; one that is more than sufficient —excessive and overflowing—a gratifying and satisfying life! So does this mean that Christians are satisfied and living the abundantly life?

The answer is found in 1 Timothy 6:6. Here we discover godliness with contentment is great gain. In other words, godliness is available without contentment. Therefore, even the godly can be living a life *without* contentment and *without* abundance. Part of our problem is lack of understanding. God tells us in Hosea 4:6 that His people are destroyed for lack of knowledge.

This is a book designed to take you on a journey for knowledge, to find instruction which when applied will result in your experiencing the abundant life of a satisfied woman. This is a book about learning to enjoy life to it's fullest potential. This is a book that will lead you to the doorway of your destiny which can only be lived to it's fullest from a place of satisfaction. This book contains the secret that will enable you to walk through any circumstance with a bounce in your step and a song in your heart, daily proclaiming "I've got satisfaction".

With the blessings found in genuinely living as a satisfied woman, I pray you will allow your life to be a witness and light of rejoicing that will bring other women to Christ where they, too, have the opportunity to learn how to obtain fulfillment and live as satisfied women.

Before continuing please turn to Appendix A at the back of the book and complete the questionnaire, *"Discovering Satisfaction"*.

In prayer I release the pages of this book as an eternal deposit from my life to yours,

Sarah Ann Goebel

CHAPTER ONE

The Dreams We Dream — Is it All Vanity?

"Everything is meaningless. What does man gain from all his labor at which he toils under the sun?"
(Ecclesiastes 1:3)

Think back to when you were fifteen years old. You were probably like many of us and you were saying, "Just as soon as I turn sixteen and can drive, I will be so happy. I will never complain about anything again." Your sixteenth birthday has come and gone. You have been driving for years now. Have you been content since that time? Why not? What happened?

Or, perhaps you have said, "When I get out of college, I'll be happy and satisfied with my life." Or, "When I get these debts paid off, I will be satisfied."

I've heard many declarations as to what would bring happiness and satisfaction to one's life – a new house, a new weight, a new shape, a larger bosom, a smaller bosom, a baby, no more babies, a college degree, a career opportunity, a better husband, a better wife (men). Think about it for a moment. If you were to have a totally satisfied life, how would you describe it? Would it require you to be taller? Shorter? Would it require you to have longer legs or a longer waistline? Maybe you are the woman who thinks, "If only we could get a larger home, I would be satisfied." Or, "As soon as I can get that new position, or that promotion that pays more with better benefits, then I will be happy." Or you may be single and thinking, "As soon as I find that man, Mr. Perfect, I will be a fully satisfied woman and will not complain about anything again." You know, Mr. Perfect.... The one who is perfect until you find out he leaves the seat up on the commode, squeezes the toothpaste on the wrong end, or snores and keeps you up all night!

What is it you picture when you picture living as a genuinely satisfied woman? Is it being married rather than being single? Or being single rather than being married? Is it having a child rather than being childless? Perhaps you are like the woman who said, "Once my earning power is equal to my yearning power, then I will be satisfied." Or do you fantasize of a life contented with your family gathering at the beach home, and the children playing together as "best friends" while you and your husband are stretched out on the beach, catching rays and listening to the sound of the ocean roar? I'll have to admit, although I have learned this is not the main key to satisfaction, it sure would be a great way to experience some R & R (rest & relaxation) and is important to a healthy life.

Where is it you find yourself today? Perhaps you think there is no way you will ever experience happiness and abundance in life because of your family heritage. Perhaps you are feeling as though life is empty and futile because nothing seems to bring lasting fulfillment. It may be that you feel about

life the way Matthew Arnold describes in his poem
"Rugby Chapel":

> Most men eddy about
> Here and there—eat and drink,
> Chatter and love and hate,
> Gather and squander, are raised
> Aloft, are hurl'd in the dust,
> Striving blindly, achieving
> Nothing; and then they die—[2]

Do you feel at times as though you labor even to
the point of exhaustion, yet never experience fulfillment? If so, you are probably viewing your life from
under the sun, meaning that you are looking at your
circumstances from a human perspective. There
is another perspective I will share with you in this
book; and it is in this perspective that you will find
the satisfied life you are seeking.

Although writing under the inspiration of the
Holy Spirit, when writing the Book of Ecclesiastes
located in the Old Testament of the Holy Bible,
Solomon wrote from a human point of view as he

tried to apply *human reasoning* to the complexities and problems of life. His conclusion was that all is vanity. Ironically, Solomon was looking at a society that was similar to today's society. There were injustices to the poor; crooked politics, incompetent leaders, guilty people allowed to continue to commit more crime, materialism, and a desire for "the good old days".[3] It doesn't sound like the world has changed much, does it? The point is that just as it was then, it is now. Circumstances, people, positions, things all change from time to time in our lives. Therefore, if we count on any of these for a satisfied life, then satisfaction is going to be a fleeting thing. It will come and go like the wind. So where is the good news for our lives?

The good news is that life can be rich and it can be a great exploration filled with satisfaction *if* you learn to draw upon the deep resources of God. Take a look at the trees. When you look at the trees, you see the *result* of the depth of their roots. The roots have been drawing the necessary resources up to strengthen and bring life to the tree above ground.

Just like the tree thrives from these hidden resources of water and minerals from beneath the earth, people thrive when by faith they draw upon the hidden resources that come from God. Without the water and minerals the tree would die from the pressures of the sun, wind, cold and heat. If we do not tap into and receive the resources of God for our lives, the pressures of life will soon cause us to fail as well. There is only one true source of satisfaction and that is God. He never changes but is the same yesterday, today and forever (Hebrews 13:8). You can know Him and you can know you are His. Without a relationship with God, genuine satisfaction is not available. This relationship with God is available only through the acceptance of the gift of salvation purchased for us by Jesus Christ of Nazareth.

It is *impossible* to find lasting satisfaction in the things of the world i.e., possessions, pleasures, power, prestige, people. But for those who belong to God, they have available to them wealth, and pleasure. God tells us in 1 Timothy 6:17, *"Command those who are rich in this present world not to be arrogant nor to put their hope in wealth, which is so uncertain, but to put their hope in God, who richly provides us with everything for our enjoyment."* As we put our hope in God, He richly gives us every-thing! And He gives it for the purpose of **our** enjoy-ment. What a great God He is! This Scripture should eradicate any beliefs you may have had that said you cannot be a Christian and have enjoyment in this life! In fact, the truth is just the opposite.

If you don't know Jesus Christ, then it is true that "all is vanity" because every thing *you do,* everything *you have* and everything *you are* will one day perish. But if you belong to Christ, you have the opportunity to invest in that which is eternal and to experience satisfaction and abundance in your life today and for all eternity. You have the opportunity as you learn to live for God's purposes, to view the things under the sun from above the sun – from God's perspective! With this increased scope of vision, you have a true perspective that can lead you to a destiny of purpose, peace and fulfillment.

ROAD STOP:

This is the first road stop along our journey for satisfaction. If you have not yet received Jesus Christ as your Lord and Savior, you will be continually searching to fill the void you find in your heart. It is a vacuum that things, people or special circumstances are not able to fill. God put the hole there and the hole is a longing that can only be filled by His presence in your life.

If you grew up in church or if you have considered yourself to be a Christian yet you find that you are always anxious and dissatisfied; or if you are not absolutely sure of your salvation, living with doubt that if you were to die today you would be with God forever, then I recommend that you take this time to confirm your salvation. You need to know for sure that you have eternal life with God. Before we continue on our journey, we will take a couple of minutes to see what the Bible says about eternal life.

CHAPTER TWO

Knowing for Sure

*"He who has the Son has the life; he who does not
have the Son of God does not have the life"*
(1 John 5:12)

❦

The Bible says, "…the GIFT of God is eternal
life through Jesus Christ our Lord" (Romans
6:23). Just like any gift, you cannot earn the gift of
eternal life. The truth is you cannot do enough good
deeds to earn salvation. Why? The bible answers this
in Romans 3:23, "All have sinned and come short of
the glory of God". God gives you this free gift even
though you have transgressed His law with sin(s)
such as lying, cheating, stealing, lusting and all kinds
of immoral thoughts and behavior. Ephesians 2:8-9
says, "for by grace are you saved through faith; and

not of yourselves; it is the GIFT of God: NOT OF WORKS, lest any one should boast. Matthew 5:48 tells us, "Be ye therefore perfect, even as your Father which is in heaven is perfect." No one can meet this standard! But God has made a way for us because of His love toward us. "…I have loved thee with an everlasting love…" (Jeremiah 31:3). "God is love" according to 1 John 4:8 and He does not want to punish us. However, God is also a Just Judge and He must punish sin. He says, "…(I) will by no means clear the guilty…" (Exodus 34:7). If you had someone to steal from you or you knew someone who had damaged your neighbor's property, yet the judge said, "Well, I like this guy so I won't punish him?" you would not see him as a just judge, would you? So God loves us, yet He has to punish sin or He would not be a just and holy God. The fall of mankind resulting in a sin nature was of no surprise to God. He had a plan to bring man into a deeper and higher level relationship with Himself through the person of Jesus Christ. The Bible tells us clearly that Jesus is the infinite GOD-MAN. "In the beginning was the Word (Jesus)…and the Word (Jesus) was God. And the Word (Jesus) was made flesh, and dwelt among us...." (John 1:1, 14). So Jesus Christ came to earth and lived a perfect and sinless life. Then He died on the cross to pay the penalty of our sins and rose from the grave so we could have eternal life with God forever. "All we like sheep have gone astray; we have turned every one to his own way; and the LORD hath laid on Him (Jesus) the transgressions (sin) of us all" (Isaiah 53:6). Jesus Christ bore our sin in His body on the cross and now offers you eternal life as a free gift.

To receive this free gift, you must have saving faith. This is different than believing there is a God and it is different than believing in Jesus as a prophet who lived some 2,000 years ago. The Bible says that the devil believes that there is one God so even to believe that will not save you. Saving faith is not trusting God for delivery in a crisis situation. We can trust God in crisis situations, however, this trust is not what gives you eternal life.

Saving faith is trusting Jesus Christ alone for eternal life. It is believing that Christ came from heaven, laid His life down as the perfect sacrifice and payment for your sins, and was resurrected from the dead unto eternal life. It is believing in the finished work of Christ alone for salvation instead of what you have done. "...Believe (trust) on the Lord Jesus Christ and thou shalt be saved...." (Acts 16:31). This is the greatest story ever told! My husband says it is the greatest deal you will ever be offered! The question now is, would you like to receive Jesus Christ – the GIFT OF ETERNAL LIFE?

You can do this by admitting you are a sinner in need of a Savior. Repent of your sins by telling God you are sorry for them and that you desire to turn from them. Tell God that you accept by faith Jesus Christ as your Savior and invite Him in to live in your heart today. He says, "Behold I stand at the door and knock: if any man hears My voice, and opens the door, I will come in to him..." (Revelation 3:20).

Receive Jesus Christ as Lord of your life by asking Him to take control of every area of your life from this day forward? He has a plan and purpose for your life and it is a good one!

"For I know the plans I have for you," declares the LORD, "plans to prosper you and not to harm you, plans to give you hope and a future"(Jeremiah 29:11). Most likely you have not been doing such a good job planning your own life. You will be glad He is now the One doing the steering!

If you want to quit trying to walk through the journey of life on your own by surrendering your life to Him now, you can do it sitting right here with this book in your hand. The Bible says, "For with the heart man believes unto righteousness; and with the mouth confession is made unto salvation. For whosoever shall call upon the name of the Lord shall be saved" (Romans 10:10, 13).

If you want to receive this gift of eternal life, then call on Jesus and ask Him for the FREE gift right now. Here is a suggested prayer: "Lord Jesus Christ, I know I am a sinner and do not deserve eternal life. But, I believe You died and rose from the grave to purchase a place in heaven for me. Lord Jesus, come into my life; take control of my life; forgive my sins and save me. I repent of my sins and now place my trust in You for my salvation. I accept the free gift of eternal life."

If you prayed this prayer as a sincere desire of your heart, you have been adopted into the family of God and you now have eternal life with Him. "Verily, verily, I say unto you, he that believeth on Me hath everlasting life" (John 6:47 KJV).

Welcome to God's family! "But as many as received Him, to them gave He power to become the sons of God, even to them that believe on His name" (John 1:12 *NKJV).*

As you grow in relationship with Christ, the Holy Spirit will reveal those things in your life that are not pleasing to Him or that He desires to change. Tell Him you are sorry and stop doing these things as He prompts you. He will give you the power you need to follow Him into the abundant life He came to give you.

You now belong to God and by surrendering your life to Him, you are in the best hands you can be in – His hands! Now you can continue on in your search for satisfaction with an *expectation* to discover it!

CHAPTER THREE

Where Not To Look

"He feeds on ashes, a deluded heart misleads him;
he cannot save himself, or say,
"Is not this thing in my right hand a lie?"
(Isaiah 44:20)

E veryone desires to be fulfilled and to feel complete, satisfied and self-sufficient. If you are like most, however, you have to admit that you have been on a quest for satisfaction your entire life. That's okay. It is a human need and every human, whether male or female, strives to find contentment in life. However, as we have discussed previously, those in the church are just as dissatisfied as those in the world. What we see is a world full of people who are restless and discontent, continually seeking for that person, place, thing, position, recognition, or change in their circumstances with a hope that this is going to be the thing that will bring them to a peaceful state of complete satisfaction, self-sufficiency and fulfillment.

Solomon in the Book of Ecclesiastes concluded at one point in his journey for satisfaction that there is no gain, no profit and no abiding value to man from his labor in this life. After all, no matter what was enjoyed or accomplished it would one day perish and the frightening shadow of death is always looming with man. Man is born and dies and the world seems not to notice. That doesn't sound too promising, does it? If that is all there is, who could find any satisfaction in this life?

Genuine satisfaction is available, but only to those who know Christ. I ask you, if you know Christ, then why are you still unsatisfied? Why is it that so many Christians are so discontent? With the promises in the Bible for an abundant life – one that is gratifying and satisfying, I found myself on a journey to answer this question.

On my quest, I discovered a very important truth. Many Christians are discontent because although they **KNOW** Christ, they do not **LOOK TO** Christ for their satisfaction. Most Christian women are deceived, just like those who do not know Christ, into looking in all the wrong places for fulfillment. They believe that they can find satisfaction in having more of something or more of someone when the only true source of satisfaction is God.

The deception comes as we receive a counterfeit sense of fulfillment. As we encounter this fleeting experience of satisfaction, the desire for that same substitute only increases and we begin to chase after that particular substitute even more. There is no end—there is no fulfillment to the desire. The desire only continues to increase more and more and we find ourselves moving in a continuous circle of desiring and receiving and wanting more – around and around we go like the merry-go-round. Only, we are not merry.

As children of God through Jesus Christ, we have access to God who is the *source* to fill that void we are trying so desperately to fill. This is the **right** place to look for *peace* and *satisfaction*—In Christ. "He has made everything beautiful in its time. He has also set eternity in the hearts of men; yet they cannot fathom what God has done from beginning to end" (Ecclesiastes 3:11). God has made us for Himself and it is only He who can satisfy us. We are told to love the Lord God with all of our heart, mind, soul and strength (Matthew 22:37). When we do this, we have taken another step towards experiencing a satisfied life, blessed with the abundance God has for us as stated in 1 Timothy 6:6, "Godliness with contentment brings great gain (abundance)." In other words, as we know God and walk in His ways, we experience the *contentment* that comes with the *freedom* that results from *understanding* that it is God who provides for us in every aspect of our lives.

I love to read the psalms. In the psalms you find trials and you find victories; you find discouragement and you find rejoicing; you find battles and you find peace; you find God's people questioning, reasoning and receiving God's answers for their circumstances.

The psalms give me hope that although I may be experiencing a difficult season, victory will triumph!

The Psalmist in Psalm 63 beautifully illustrates to us how we are to love God in order that we may live a rich and satisfied life. Here the psalmist exemplifies my picture of a true worshipper of God as he finds his soul's satisfaction in God. The soul that is satisfied is the one that loves God with all of His heart, mind, soul and strength. He is totally involved in worshipping God as seen in the psalmist.

We see him worship God with his eyes in verse 2, "Early will I seek You"; with his lips in verse 3b," My lips shall praise You"; with his hands in verse 4b, "I will lift up my hands in Your name"; with his soul in verse 5, "My soul shall be satisfied as with marrow and fatness"; with his mouth in verse 5b, "And my mouth shall praise You with joyful lips"; and with his mind in verse 6, "I meditate on You in the night watches." He says in verse 63:5, "my soul shall be satisfied as with marrow and fatness." The psalmist is speaking of the richest of foods in these verses. He is talking about rich chocolate pie like my mom use to make and rich custard pudding. None of that diet stuff for the psalmist. We should not be starving for soul satisfaction either. He is saying that his soul shall be content and satisfied to the richest possibility. It is so true, my friends. A genuine, rich satisfaction is available to us who (1) know God and who (2) worship Him with every part of our lives.

We read in Psalm 16:11, "In your presence is *fullness* of joy." Standing in the presence of our God, we experience a *fullness* of joy where there is not even a trace of discontentment. It is here that the abundant life of worth, peace, fulfillment and joy are found.

We see Jesus in John 15:11 speaking to His disciples and saying, "These things have I spoken unto you, that My joy might remain in you, and that your joy might be full." We see that those of us who have accepted Christ as our Lord and Saviour have the *opportunity* to live our lives satisfied in the fullness of joy. Why? The answer is *because of Christ.*

Yet, although the opportunity is here, I look around and I see the majority of people walking through this journey on earth as discontented, unhappy individuals who wonder if satisfaction is something illusive and unobtainable. I see Christian women with long faces and complaining attitudes; and some are walking through life as if all is hopeless. How can this be? Let's take another look at the *salvation* experience and compare to the *realities of satisfaction* in relationship to the world and to the church.

Salvation is a gift of God and *we receive it by faith*. We do not seek it out. God chose us; opened our eyes that we could see Him and choose Him and He saved us. Ephesians 2:8-9 tells us that salvation is a free gift, not of works that any man can boast. What a great love He has for us!

This is **not** true about satisfaction. Satisfaction is NOT received by faith and it DOES NOT come to us at the point of salvation. It is not instantaneous and it is not found without works. Yes, we are saved without works, but God has left this hole in our souls so we would hunger and thirst for Him. He desires us to run towards Him, seek Him out and spend time with Him.

Any thing you try as a substitute in the place of God will run straight through you like water through a sieve. It will not stick! It's like trying to stay full on one of those liquid diets. You soon find yourself empty looking for some person or some thing to bring fulfillment to your life. This is the explanation for the void in our souls and this is the reason that it can only be filled by God Himself.

You can be saved YET not experience satisfaction, BUT you can't experience satisfaction without first being saved (through experiencing Jesus Christ as Lord and Savior). Salvation is by faith and without works. Satisfaction is by knowledge and requires work. We are told in Colossians 3:1 that we are to set our affections on God! To look for satisfaction in any other place; in any other way, is idolatry and not only does it fail, but it will lead to even more dissatisfaction. Isaiah 44:20 describes to us what happens when we fall into idolatry. "He feeds on ashes, a deluded heart misleads him; he cannot save himself, or say, "Is not this thing in my right hand a lie?" We begin to crave and desire more of a thing as if it is going to satisfy us even though it has not satisfied us as yet. We are unable to recognize that this money, place, position, person, thing is deceiving us. When you begin living for the world instead of for God's purposes, your perspective on life changes and the result is disappointment.

ROAD STOP:

Take a moment here and think honestly about yourself. Do you find yourself desiring more and more of some THING in your life and yet never feel like you have had enough? It could be money, success, more things, etc. If so, you have a *deluded heart* and these *things* are holding you *captive*. Repent and set your mind on Christ and be set free!

Now, let's take a more in-depth look at the world's view of contentment.

CHAPTER FOUR

A World's View of Satisfaction

"They have harps and lyres at their banquets, tambourines and flutes and wine, but they have no regard for the deeds of the LORD, no respect for the work of his hands" (Isaiah 5:12)

The definition for satisfaction according to <u>The American Heritage College Dictionary</u> is a) The fulfillment or gratification of a desire, need, or appetite and b) Pleasure or contentment derived from such gratification.[4]

Isaiah 5:12 puts it like this, "They have harps and lyres at their banquets, tambourines and flutes and wine, but they have no regard for the deeds of the LORD, no respect for the work of his hands."

Contentment from a world's view is the possessing of, the indulging in, the hoarding of, or the obtaining of something *outside* of oneself. The world's view of contentment teaches us that we receive contentment from people: "If I could just hang out with the right people." But people never live up to our expectations. The world teaches that contentment comes from positions we hold. "If I could just get the right job, that allows me to make the good income, drive a nice car, live in a nice house, I would be content." But what happens when we don't get the job or the company closes down and we lose it?

The woman who lives by the world's view of satisfaction is living with highs and lows because her level of satisfaction is affected by *external sources* such as people, position and material items — all subject to change.

A popular American expression speaks of 'keeping up with the Joneses,' that is, having as many material possessions as your neighbors. In the race to see who can outdo who, contentment is becoming extinct even in the lives of those in the Church. Johnny gets the newly released cell phone model with all the bells and whistles; so Paul watches anxiously for the next newest release in order to upstage Johnny, even though the one he has works perfectly.

The world feeds our self-centered desires with a constant bombardment of advertising from bill-boards, the internet, and television commercials. All these advertisements promise us "happiness" but focus our attention on ourselves and our wants to such a level that our *NOT having it* causes us unhap-piness, un-fulfillment and depression. 1 Timothy 6 tells us that the pursuit of things at all costs, results in grief.

In Ecclesiastes 3:11 we read God has put "eter-nity in their heart and nobody can find peace and satisfaction apart from Him." He has put a spiritual yearning in your heart that can only be filled by the Eternal One. We try to fill it with substitutes that come in many different forms. If you live by faith in yourself and what *you can do* or by faith in someone else and what *they can do for you*, or by faith in any thing and what *it can do for you,* you will be disappointed. Again, the experience of satisfaction derived from any source other than God is counterfeit and will disappoint you, deceive you and slowly begin to hold you captive. The results of the captivity will be a seeking after that substitute(s) more and more in search of genuine satisfaction. But will you find it? No you won't. Instead, you will find that you are returning once again to that familiar place of emptiness. And so the cycle continues. A cycle of deception that enslaves you and holds you in bondage to some idol that cannot bring satisfaction but only brings dissatisfaction to your soul. In this state, although you are saved, the truly abundant life God has for you lies off in the distance somewhere.

Look again at Isaiah 5:12 along with Isaiah 5:13, "They have harps and lyres at their banquets, tambourines and flutes and wine, but they have no regard for the deeds of the LORD, no respect for the work of his hands." Now verse 12, "Therefore my people will go into exile for lack of understanding; their men of rank will die of hunger and their masses will be parched with thirst." Their music and alcohol is a *counterfeit experience of satisfaction* and *comes to an end*. Genuine satisfaction on the other hand, *cannot* be changed from external sources. Genuine satisfaction is **internal** and **eternal**.

To summarize the world's view of satisfaction, it is like most everything else in the world. It is based on SELF. It is about me getting what "I" want and doing what "I" want, even though it only results in temporary satisfaction. "Even in laughter the heart may ache, and joy may end in grief" (Proverbs 14:13). In this state of dissatisfaction, one cannot experience true abundance or the fullness of the destiny God has for them. So if satisfaction is not based on the world's view which is self-centered, what is it based on? We will look at the basis for genuine satisfaction in the next chapter.

ROAD STOP:

Do you find yourself caught up in materialism and trying to keep up with the Joneses? What are some ways you could try to avoid this trap?

What are some of the substitutes you find yourself looking to in search of satisfaction? It could include anything that brings you a sense of significance, acceptance, power, importance or worthiness outside of your relationship with God.

Tell God you are sorry for committing this sin of idolatry and putting these things or these people in His place. Ask Him to forgive you. Then by faith you can accept that He has forgiven you and believe that He has cleansed you from all unrighteousness (1 John 1:9).

CHAPTER FIVE

The Biblical View of Satisfaction

"I am not saying this because I am in need, for I have learned to be content whatever the circumstances" (Philippians 4:11)

When scripture speaks of being content, it is speaking of being wholly complete and sufficient—physically, emotionally and spiritually—needing absolutely nothing. The Holman Bible Dictionary puts it like this; "an internal satisfaction which does not demand changes in external circumstances".[5] Can you imagine a person like this? It is plain to see in the book of Philippians that Paul was one of these people. He says in Philippians 4:11, "I am not saying this because I am in need, for I have learned to be content whatever the circumstances."

A lesson to obtain from this passage is that Paul is willing to accept those things he cannot change. He is willing to accept the life that God has given him. You say, "But Sarah, I am in a marriage with an unbeliever who is rude and has the worst personality on the face of this earth. He is impossible to live with." Or you say, "Sarah, I have been falsely persecuted and lied about. How can I accept that?" Hebrews 13:15 exhorts us to depend on God's promise not to forsake His people. "Through Jesus, therefore, let us continually offer to God a sacrifice of praise—the fruit of lips that confess his name" (Heb 13:15). As Christians, we can choose to live by faith *in ourselves and the circumstances* that surround us or we can live by faith *in a Sovereign, all-powerful and loving God!* We need *not* be concerned about our past which cannot be changed and we need *not* focus on our circumstances of today. Why? God has ordained that we live by faith and not by sight. Our God is a God of redemption and restoration and we can trust Him to redeem and restore. Just as He restored the loss of children, possessions and health to Job in the

Book of Job, He can restore our losses as well. "After Job had prayed for his friends, the LORD made him prosperous again and gave him twice as much as he had before" (Job 42:10). As we ***trust*** in God and His sovereignty, we are ***enabled*** to persevere. "*Indeed we count them blessed who endure. You have heard of the perseverance of Job and seen the end intended by the Lord—that the Lord is very compassionate and merciful*" (James 5:11 NKJV).

God will even take our mistakes and make good of them when we love Him and are called according to His purposes (Romans 8:28) just as He did with Rahab the Harlot. One day when the Israelites sent spies into Jericho to see how they might take the city, she was presented with an opportunity to help them. She had heard about the power of the Israelites' God and how He favored them. She believed they would, indeed, be successful on their mission in Jericho, so she boldly proclaimed her faith in their God and she made a deal to hide the spies in exchange for her and her family's life. As a result of her faith in God, Rahab and her family were saved during a crisis where there seemed to be no way out. She married an Israelite and became an ancestor of the Lord Jesus Christ. She is one of only two women who God has listed in what we call the "hall of faith chapter", Chapter 11 of the Book of Hebrews. Not only do we see God making good out of what appeared to be impossible circumstances, but we see God made good out of Rahab's past reputation as He brought her from a harlot to an ancestor of Christ. God can redeem life from your past too!

Look at the story of Joseph in Genesis 35-50. Joseph was given a dream – you might say a Word from the Lord. In the dream he was ruling over his brothers. Joseph's brothers were jealous of him and after hearing of the dream, they hated him all the more. One day they sold him into slavery. Joseph was purchased from the slave traders by an Egyptian official and he prospered as a servant in his house. The official's wife accused him of trying to rape her and Joseph ended up in a prison for a crime he did not commit. But even while waiting on God in that prison, the favor of God was on him. All that he put his hand to do was blessed. One day, several years later, Joseph interpreted a dream for the Pharoah who then put him in charge of the whole land of Egypt. Joseph became the second most powerful man next to the Pharoah. There was a terrible famine in the land that lasted seven years just as Joseph had shared would happen and Joseph's brothers came to Egypt seeking food for their family. It was unknown to them that they were seeking help from their brother whom they had sold into slavery. Joseph's brothers repented when they discovered the identity of their brother and they bowed down to him. Joseph's family was saved from the famine because of the position of authority God had exalted Joseph to. Joseph proclaims to his brothers, "But as for you, you meant evil against me; but God meant it for good, in order to bring it about as it is this day, to save many people alive" (Genesis 50:20 NKJV). God is sovereign and He will use what is meant for evil against us for His good purposes. God has given us promises that we are to stand on, trusting Him in His own timing to bring them to pass.

In the book of Philippians, we see that Paul was in prison and yet he rejoiced. He was content to know that God was in charge and in knowing what God had done for Him. He trusted the *character* of God and the *sovereignty* of God concerning what lay ahead in his eternal future. Paul *willed* to be content and *carried his will out* in his actions. You see, satisfaction begins with our **acceptance of God's plan** for us no matter what the circumstance involved; no matter what people or things are there or are lacking; no matter what.

In contrast with the world's view of satisfaction, to walk out the Biblical definition of satisfaction requires full dependence on what is on the inside of a woman. Just as Paul learned the secret of contentment through his experiences of trials and blessings, you can be initiated into this secret as well. As a Christian woman, you have the same power residing within you as did Paul, and *it is this power of Christ within that gives spiritual satisfaction*. Philippians 4:12-13, "I know what it is to be in need, and I know what it is to have plenty. I have learned the secret of being content in any and every situation, whether well fed or hungry, whether living in plenty or in want. I can do everything through him who gives me strength." You see it is this hidden part of the Christian life that only God sees that is the most important part of all. It is there that all the power needed to adequately meet the demands of life exists. All we need to do is trust God, release our faith and look for the blessings in our each and every day.

ROAD STOP:

Ask God to help you recognize and experience the power of Christ within that brings genuine satisfaction. Begin to release that power into your life every morning as you rise. You are empowered by Christ who dwells in you to meet every challenge of life.

Is what is happening around you as important as your attitude concerning it? Let your faith be a rudder to steer you into calmer waters.

Can you think of situations in your life that God has saved you from? Make a list and refer back to it as a reminder during times when your faith is weak.

CHAPTER SIX

The Secret of Joy

*"These things have I spoken unto you, that My joy
may remain in you, and that your joy may be full"
(John 15:11 NKJV)*

B efore Jesus faced the cruel and undeserved
punishment and death of Calvary, He said to
His followers, "These things have I spoken unto you,
that My joy might remain in you, and that your joy
might be full" (John 15:11). How could he speak of
joy at a time like that?

Jesus, although a man acquainted with grief, had
a satisfaction with his life that was beyond anything
the world could offer. Even as He faced a horrible
death He could be content. Jesus desired that His
followers possess this same kind of satisfaction in

their lives. In Psalm 16:11, we are told we can have fullness of joy because we belong to God. Christians can be free from living discontented, unfulfilled lives. God will equip His children to receive genuine joy and satisfaction in the place of *discontent, greed,* and *covetousness.*

When I think about discontentment, my thoughts go back to the story of Naomi and Ruth found in Ruth 1:16-22. At a time when Bethlehem was struck with famine, Naomi and her family who were Israelites, were forced to move from there. They settled in the land called Moab where the people worshipped a false god called Chemosh. Naomi had two sons, one of which married a Moabite woman named Ruth. Naomi's husband and two sons died and after being gone from Bethlehem for several years, Naomi decides to return. She tells Ruth to stay behind but Ruth insists on honoring Naomi, staying by her mother-in-law's side even though Naomi had not been the most pleasant woman to be with since her husband and sons had died. Her discontent with what God had allowed in her life turned to bitterness as seen by her response when they entered the city and the women there excitedly asked "Can this be Naomi" (Ruth 1:19)? Naomi responded, "Don't call me Naomi." "Call me Mara, because the Almighty has made my life very bitter. I went away full, but the LORD has brought me back empty. Why call me Naomi? The LORD has afflicted me; the Almighty has brought misfortune upon me" (Ruth 1:20-21). Naomi chose for herself a name which meant "bitter" during this season of her life where she was overshadowed with sorrow rather than choosing to maintain an attitude of joy as the name Naomi means "my joy". Naomi failed to understand the character of God in the midst of her loss. Had she understood God had an eternal purpose for her life, she could have maintained her joy through these circumstances while she *waited for God's plan to unfold.* You see, God did come through with His plan and the purpose was revealed in His bringing Naomi and Ruth to Bethlehem. Ruth began to work as a gleaner in the barley fields of a relative of Naomi's who was called Boaz, and Boaz eventually took Ruth as his wife. A child, Obed, was born to Ruth and Naomi cared for him. Naomi's joy was restored because of her daughter in law's faithfulness to what God had put before her—her mother in law. The women said to Naomi: "Praise be to the LORD, who this day has not left you without a kinsman-redeemer. May he become famous throughout Israel! He will renew your life and sustain you in your old age. For your daughter-in-law, who loves you and who is better to you than seven sons, has given him birth" (Ruth 4:14-15). Obed became the father of Jesse, and Jesse the father of King David. What an awesome God! We can maintain our joy in every circumstance knowing that God is in control and has a purpose for all He allows into our lives. We can know that although we may not *see it* or *understand it*, God has a *purpose in it* and His purposes play into His eternal plan.

The four short chapters in the book of Philippians will change your life if you can capture the principles of Paul's inward joy shared throughout those pages. Your life will never be the same. Discontent and complaining thoughts will soon disappear. As you study the book of Philippians, you will find that Paul was beaten and in prison and His very life was in danger. The possibility of being beheaded overshadowed his days. How could he freely minister and write with an attitude of joy and contentment? How could he *continue on* with his work in the midst of those extremely difficult circumstances?

Paul lived with joy in his life despite his *present circumstances* and despite his *past*. The fact that his past was spotted with the sin of persecuting Christians even unto death would have caused most Christians to believe God could not use them. But Paul lived his life according to Philippians 3:13-14, "Brothers, I do not consider myself yet to have taken hold of it. But one thing I do: *Forgetting what is behind and straining toward what is ahead,* I press on toward the goal to win the prize for which God has called me heavenward in Christ Jesus." For Paul, the secret to overcoming discontentment was to *focus His attention on the **purposes of God*** in his life. There was nothing he could do about the past, so he did not let himself become concerned about that. Rather, Paul focused on what God was calling him to do *RIGHT NOW* so that he would fulfill the purposes of God IN THE FUTURE. Don't be distracted by your circumstances. "Have faith in God and like Ruth, *do* those things you *know to do* today. In other words, be *faithful to the assignment* He has given you for this season – *help others* and with joy watch God fulfill His plan through the circumstances of your life. James 2:26 says, "For as the body without the spirit is dead, so faith without works is dead also." It is your faith in God *revealed* in your actions that **empowers** you to live a life of joy and satisfaction.

ROAD STOP:

Are you still focusing on failures of the past? Are you focusing on where you came from? It is time to let go of the past and focus on where God has you at today. Realize that He is working out His plan for your life. Therefore, focus on what He is calling you to do in *today's* circumstances that will enable you to walk into the purposes God has for your *future*.

CHAPTER SEVEN

Joy in the Midst

*"What is more, I consider everything a loss
compared to the surpassing greatness of knowing
Christ Jesus my Lord, for whose sake
I have lost all things. I consider them rubbish,
that I may gain Christ" (Philippians 3:8)*

Have you ever looked at life and thought about how little control you have over your circumstances? Think about it. Did you have any control concerning the time of your conception; or when you were brought into the world? No, of course you didn't. Did you choose who your parents would be? No you did not. You had no control concerning any of these things. Look at your life while growing up and you will discover you had little or no control over most things that went on in your life. For instance, did you choose the school you attended, where you lived, how your family celebrated holidays? How about your present circumstances? How much control do you actually have over them? Look at the weather today. Do you have control over whether it will rain or the sun will shine? Perhaps like my brother, you worked for a large manufacturing plant that shut down. Suddenly he found himself out of work. How much control do you have over circumstances?

There are many circumstances that you have zero control over. Therefore, it is impossible to be a satisfied woman if you are depending on *ideal circumstances.* Ideal circumstances present themselves in our lives on occasion but, *for the most part we are faced with changes and faced with circumstances that are out of our control.*

Paul recognized he was not in control of his circumstances, but he knew Someone who was. He discovered the secret of joy and satisfaction was *not to depend* on his circumstances. He was able to be content no matter what because he had learned to cultivate a mindset that said, "To live is Christ and to die is gain". Without cultivating a **yielded mind** to Christ — without CHOOSING to *believe* and *receive* and *obey* what God says and allows as a Sovereign God, your circumstances will deprive you of your satisfaction.

Paul believed and lived out the truth that nothing else matters in comparison to the promise we have in Christ Jesus. Philippians 3:8, "What is more, I consider everything a loss compared to the surpassing greatness of knowing Christ Jesus my Lord, for whose sake I have lost all things. I consider them rubbish that I may gain Christ". Because he made a decision to live for Christ and to accept what Jesus said as being true, Paul was able to keep his eyes on the Lord and the eternal promises Jesus had shown him. This mindset enabled Paul to tap into the power of God so that he experienced beatings, stoning, jailing, shipwreck, hunger, desertion, misunderstanding and more without losing his joy.

Things happen in our lives, both good things and things that are difficult to handle. The same was true in Paul's life. Paul was a man who desired to preach in Rome, yet he found himself in prison, unable to preach publicly. Even worse was the possibility of being beheaded! Yet he ministered to those who were around him as a man who was completely content. He wrote a letter to the Philippians that proclaimed an attitude of *acceptance of the circumstances **God** had placed him in*. Paul was not complaining. He was joyful and satisfied with his life, even while in prison.

Some prisons don't have bars and locked doors. Perhaps you are in a job that you feel trapped in. Or, perhaps your marriage is on the rocks and you find yourself desiring to run away from it. You made a commitment and you believe God intended for marriage to be until death do us part, but you feel as though you are imprisoned in a very difficult situation. Many women flee from these marriages, saying, "God doesn't want me to be miserable." They may even run into the imprisonment of another similar marriage. But you see God is more concerned about your *holiness* than your *happiness*.[6] I am not saying that God would want a woman to stay in an abusive environment where her life may be endangered.

However, *sometimes we feel like we are in prison just because we don't have things our way and we don't realize that God has put us in this place to refine us.* A mind YIELDED to God will say "Lord whatever it takes — make me like you."

As a mother, I one day found myself faced with the challenge of raising two young teenagers alone. This was not my decision. I did not choose it for my life. In fact, I had always dreamed of living happily ever after as a wife and mother. I dreamed of living in the house with the little white picket fence. I know some of you reading this book had the same dream. However, here I was in a circumstance out of my control *beyond my ability to change.*

Although I had no power over the circumstance itself, I did have the power to *choose how I would respond to it.* I could stay in utter depression, consider myself a failure, be miserable the rest of my life and set an example to my children of quitting on life while singing a tune of "woe is me". That was one option. Or I could pick myself up by the grace of God and hit the road to find a job that would provide for us. I chose the second option! I began a job search and discovered there was no job to be found that paid enough to support us with my high school education. But after much determination and perseverance, God eventually gave me an idea that brought in thousands of dollars a month. My children were raised with an attitude that all things work together to their good as they trust in God. They witnessed what it means to overcome even in the midst of what most people would consider very unfavorable circumstances.

The only way we can truly handle the extreme difficulties of life and maintain satisfaction is by having an attitude of submission to Christ. When we learn to live our lives with a yielded mind, *Christ is what matters most to us.* Christ was Paul's life. Paul was surrendered to Him in mind and body. He fully trusted God's plan for his life. This is what it means to have a **yielded mind** or a **yielded attitude.** Paul commented that he had only one desire and that was that Christ be exalted in his body whether by life or by death. He was saying, "Lord, whatever you want to do with me is just fine. I know you have a purpose and I am with you. I submit to you. If I live, praise the Lord. If I die, praise the Lord."

How could Paul say these things? Because for him to live was Christ and to die was gain. He was able to accept his circumstances with contentment because he knew God — *His character* and *His ways* — and he knew he could trust God no matter what.

Before Jon and I received the call to prepare for full time ministry, we were blessed with material blessings, able to do most anything that we wanted, able to buy most anything we wanted. We were blessed and we were satisfied physically, materially and spiritually. However, shortly after selling our business in obedience to the Lord, we entered a season of trial and temptation. Life-threatening illness struck both my parents and me all in one year. Finances dwindled away to nothing, and material possessions were lost. That was the *trial.*

The *temptation* was to believe the lie Satan was trying to feed us that God's Word is not true and we should turn away from Him and abandon the path He had set us on. In fact, if we looked at our *new* circumstances, it did not make sense to believe that we would be able to complete ministry training let alone have finances for full-time ministry. It seemed foolish to think that anyone could believe in us enough to sponsor us to plant and pastor a church. Our circumstances had changed drastically, but we chose to *reject the lie* of Satan and *continue trusting God.*

The consequence of our decision to trust God was that we began to experience what it means to *walk by faith and not by sight.* Did fear and disappointment try to overtake us? Of course it did. Did we cry? We cried many times. But we believed God's Word and we trusted that He is faithful. We believed God's Word when He said although sorrow may come for the night; joy will come in the morning. Therefore, turning back or quitting were not options. We set our eyes on Christ and we walked through the hard time *doing those things we knew to do*, with an *expectation* of receiving the reward Christ promised us for believing Him.

Christ must be our life. As we walk through the circumstances of life hand in hand with Jesus, we come to know that He loves us and He is in control of all things. We come to know that He is faithful and all that He promises awaits us as we put our trust in Him. *This knowledge gives us a security that can be found nowhere else.*

The Christian walk is indeed a walk of faith and not of sight. We need to order our lives *according to our faith in God and His character*, not according to what we see in our circumstances. Joni Erickson Tada is in a kind of prison because of the condition of her body. She became paralyzed from the neck down after a diving accident as a teenager. But Joni has joy despite her physical circumstances. How can she be satisfied with her life with these conditions? Her joy certainly does not come by choosing to fight against Christ! Rather, Joni has chosen to submit to what God has allowed to happen in her life. She looks forward to the day when she will see Jesus face to face, but until then she is content to glorify God through her paralysis.

We need to understand that we can be content in spite of painful and trying experiences. We can cry tears of sadness and grief and know deep peace and satisfaction at the same time. It is possible to have a deep, abiding spiritual satisfaction that never leaves us only because of our trust in God. We need to cultivate a **yielded mind** toward Christ and allow Him, not our circumstances, to be Lord of our future. We *accept Christ's sovereignty* and *turn the control of our lives over to Him*. We make a *conscious decision* that we will no longer allow circumstances to deprive us of our joy. This attitude is easy to maintain when Christ is first in our life. The yielded mind is *vital* to being a satisfied woman.

ROAD STOP:

Is Christ at the center of your life? Or is your career or ministry your primary focus in life? Who or what has first place in your life? If any person, including your husband, is the center of your life, what will happen when they let you down or fail to measure up to your expectations?

Every human being is going to fail eventually, so what happens when the person you have put first in your life fails you? Your children may disappoint you, friends may let you down, your job can be lost, and people may not appreciate your attempts to help them. Only the Love of God living on the inside of you never fails, never changes, and therefore can always be depended upon.

CHAPTER EIGHT

People and Satisfaction

*"What causes fights and quarrels among you?
Don't they come from your desires that battle within
you? You want something but don't get it. You kill
and covet, but you cannot have what you want.
You quarrel and fight. You do not have,
because you do not ask God" (James 4:1-2)*

S ometimes we allow **people** to deprive us of satisfaction – but we must give them permission to do so before this thievery can happen.[9] How do we give permission? I have discovered that we set ourselves up for this when we put *our* expectations on people – when we expect people to act, react, respond, think or do what *we* think they should do, and to be what *we* think they should be. Our own unrealistic expectations set us up for disappointment and our satisfaction is lost.

I have always been and remain to be a "people lover" but, people can rob me of satisfaction and joy if I allow them to do so by putting my expectations on them. Before ministry, I had my own business and employed people. You can believe I had ample opportunity to lose my joy and satisfaction. In fact, I did lose it because at that time I did not understand this principle of not putting our own expectations on others, but allowing them to be who God created them to be.

Walking with and assisting my husband who is senior pastor at our church, has also given me ample opportunity to allow people to have an influence on my joy and satisfaction. If you are in church, you know that the church is made up of people who are at various places in their spiritual development. Everyone in the church has not necessarily discovered that it is to their best interest to make Christ and the advancement of His kingdom their focus. Just as you and I, they are in process and none are yet perfect. In fact, the universal church has many wounded souls whom God is healing and sanctifying. Sometimes during this process people are focused on the wrong things. They may be focused on themselves which often results in being easily offended. They may be focused on their own desires and some may have trouble submitting to the decisions of leadership when it is not in agreement with their thoughts on a given situation. The truth is, we are all born into this world self-centered, and we find many are still looking for satisfaction in all the wrong places, in all the wrong ways according to their different degrees of self-centeredness.

I have heard several unchurched people call those in the church hypocrites. Please try to understand. It is not that we are hypocrites so much as it is that *we are still in process*. We realize we can not save ourselves and that we need a Saviour. We all have a relationship with Christ but the level of relationship varies from person to person. We are saved but our minds have yet to be fully renewed and the transformation has not yet fully taken place. Our spirits were born again but our minds were not. Our minds still have to be brought into alignment with the Word of God and that takes a willingness and effort on the part of each individual. Some submit to the process more quickly than others. Romans 7:24-25 says, "What a wretched man I am! Who will rescue me from this body of death? Thanks be to God – through Jesus Christ our Lord! So then, I myself in my mind am a slave to God's law, but in the sinful nature a slave to the law of sin." This Scripture is saying that I serve God in my spirit but my body is controlled by my thoughts which have not come into complete agreement with the Word of God. In order for my actions to line up with God's ways, my thinking has to be transformed, and that is a process. It doesn't happen overnight.

Therefore, you still see the world and it's mind-sets in the church. You see imperfections. And you see the members sometimes offended because they are still young in their spiritual maturity level. As we grow spiritually, we learn to talk things out and to forgive. Our focus is not to have our own way or to prove ourselves right. But it is on what God desires –

reconciliation, maintaining unity and pressing onward with our mission as the body of Christ. In addition, because of insecurities, past emotional wounds, low self esteem, and other unresolved soul issues, many Christians continue to make poor choices in their lives and demonstrate behavior that is not appropriate for a person who is aspiring to be like Christ. *The depth of the **hunger you have for Christ** plus the **amount of time spent reading and studying His word** will determine where you are in the sanctification process.* Those who choose to put on the mind of Christ by coming into agreement with what the Bible says will be stable in their faith no matter what people or circumstances they encounter in their lives. They learn to apply Philippians 4:8 to their situations involving people. *"Finally, brothers, whatever is true, whatever is noble, whatever is right, whatever is pure, whatever is lovely, whatever is admirable—if anything is excellent or praiseworthy—think about such things."* If a Christian has not progressed forward in the process of sanctification, no matter how many years they have been saved, they may still be walking, living and reacting according to their old, PRE-SALVATION mindset. They may be stuck in old habit patterns that **create pain** for themselves and often cause pain for other people in their lives as well. But be of good cheer. God has promised to perfect us all, and He will be faithful to complete what He has started in each one of us. The process will not be complete until we meet Him face to face, but those who submit to the process with a surrendering of their lives to Him will be walking on a spiritual level that those who do not cannot understand. Therefore, until we stand before Christ, purpose in your heart you will need to give people *lots of grace* in place of *your expectations*. This way you will not be robbed of your joy, and your satisfaction in life will remain intact. Allow others to be who God has made them to be and you can wait patiently for Him to perfect them in His Own time and in His Own way according to their cooperation with Him.

As I write this, my mind drifts back to last fall when my husband and I were returning back to the states from a trip to the GCI Missions School in

Romania. We landed in Italy and boarded a new jet whose destination was New York City. As we taxied to the runway, we suddenly heard the pilot's voice come over the speakers. He told us that we were taxiing off the runway due to a discovered malfunction with the aircraft. Well, I was praising the Lord. Thank God they discovered the problem **before** we took off! Some people began complaining almost instantly while others waited a while, but I was saying, "Praise God. Whatever it takes to fix it, we want this plane fixed while we are still on the ground!"

After 3 hours of sitting on the plane, not in a more comfortable terminal, you can imagine the frustration every one was feeling. When we finally got the green light from the mechanics, we took off for the long flight to New York. But, when we reached New York we discovered more problems. You probably guessed it – we had missed our connecting flight. In fact, our plane left 45 minutes before we arrived. I think I might have been a little bit too proud of my earlier perceived level of patience before takeoff.

We reached the attendant at the gate where we were to connect with our next flight. After standing in line for 30 minutes, we handed her our tickets and told her we had missed the connecting flight due to late arrival on another plane. She looked at our tickets and, after searching the computer base, she told us that she was not able to help us. "Not able to help us?" I questioned, "You mean that you don't have procedures in place for when this kind of thing happens?" I was sure we were not the first people to miss a connecting flight due to their plane being late! She called someone else over to help her. But they didn't know how to help us either. I was tired and it had been a long trip. Now they were telling us that we were stuck at the JFK airport in New York City! If they didn't know how to get us home, who did? I could feel my patience leaving and my temperature rising.

I said, "Honey…" Jon interrupted me. He suspected what I was about to say so He said, "Sarah, just be patient. Everything will be all right." You guessed it – I had lost my satisfaction! But that was not the worst of it. They sent us on a trip across the airport. Have you been to the JFK airport? It is humongous and we were pulling large suitcases with us all over the airport! We had to go outside, up and down hills, back inside, up in the elevator, on the train and finally we arrived at our destination. It seemed like we had traveled to another city! As we approached the counter I happily exclaimed, "Hallelujah!" There was no line. We handed the attendant our tickets. We told her our dilemma and that the people at the ticket counter for our connection flight had sent us here to get the problem solved. The satisfaction of being able to walk straight up to the counter without waiting suddenly left as I heard her say, "Why did they send you to me? They are not supposed to do that. I am here all by myself. They need to take care of you down there!"

She began to pick up the phone to call them while instructing us to return to where we began. Oh my goodness! She was the only one there! She had no customers to assist but us! Was this not her job? Why couldn't she help us? I was frustrated and I let her rob me of my contentment. At the same time, I knew

God was allowing this whole circumstance because I still needed some refinement in this area. I saw that I was putting my expectations on her as to how she should conduct herself with the airline customers. I became disappointed in her and I lost my joy and I lost my satisfaction.

How about you? How about when another driver pulls out in front of you and you almost hit him? Sometimes you wonder if these people are even qualified to be behind the wheel of a car! How about the cashier who is having a great time conversing with the customer in line in front of you while you are running late for a meeting? How about your husband? Your children? Your co-workers? Do you find yourself upset with them because you think they should *be* and *do* what you picture them *as* and *doing*? Sometimes as parents we expect our 3-year old to behave as a 5-year old. We put our unrealistic expectations on them and we find ourselves frustrated and angry, unable to enjoy our children. Every day, in all your relationships and in living out life, you have opportunities to put your expectations on others. If you do, those expectations can rob you of your patience, joy and of your satisfaction for the moment, the day or forever.

What are you going to do if you have a friend who betrays you? Will you still maintain an attitude of joy and satisfaction? Isn't it amazing that we turn to others to discover our worth? Isn't it amazing that we give them the power to control joy and contentment in our lives? We allow their perspective, which is at least as limited and darkened as our own, to affect us in how we see ourselves. We allow their choices to affect us — thinking that somehow their choice to do evil against us has to do with some lack in us. Would it not be wiser instead to rely on God's unchanging and encouraging reassurance? God so loved us that He gave His Son for us. How significant we are! How valuable we are! The Creator of all that is has made us according to the counsel of His Will for His good pleasure and purpose. There is no greater Source to receive our significance from. He made us and He saw that it was good!

When I think about Christ and how He must have felt when Judas betrayed Him; how He must have felt when Peter denied Him, it amazes me that He remained content. He was content because He knew God was in control and that it was God's plan that was being worked out through the lives of these people. Consider the ridicule and mocking of the soldiers and the people. Jesus asked the Father to forgive them. He experienced pain but He never lost the satisfaction of knowing that His life's purpose was playing out as He hung on that cross. God's mind was His mind and *His thoughts were on serving God and on the reward of His suffering – you and me!* How about you? Are your thoughts on God and things above or are you more concerned about your earthly rewards than your eternal ones?

We have no control over others. They will make their decisions and you have no control over what they will do or how they will feel. Some will like you. Some will not. Some may even try to hurt you and falsely persecute you. They persecuted Jesus and they persecuted Paul. Why wouldn't you and I as His followers be persecuted too?

The best way to prevent the actions of people toward us from affecting our emotions is to *make Christ's attitude our attitude.* In order to do this, you must know what Christ's attitude was like. We are told in Philippians 2:5-8, *"Your attitude should be the same as that of Christ Jesus: Who, being in very nature God, did not consider equality with God something to be grasped, but made himself nothing, taking the very nature of a servant, being made in human likeness. And being found in appearance as a man, he humbled himself and became obedient to death—even death on a cross!"*

Jesus is God and yet He took upon Himself the form of a servant and became a **bondservant** of love.

Paul identifies himself as a bondservant in the book of Philippians. The Greek word for bondservant is "doulos". Paul identified himself as one with the characteristics of a bondservant as described in Deuteronomy, Chapter 15. A bondservant was a servant who was bought for a price, but was given freedom by his master. He could have acquired his freedom but instead chose to remain a slave forever because he loved his master. By his own choice, therefore, and not by coercion, he would serve his master's household for the rest of his life. A bondservant surrendered his will to his master's will.

Paul was saying that he too had been bought with a price, but he was bound to Jesus by the bonds of love, not of duty or coercion. It was his desire that his will be swallowed up by his Master's. It was his joy that Christ be exalted in his body.

A bondservant does not have his focus on himself. His focus is on **His Master**. A bondservant regards others more important than himself. When you have the attitude of a *servant* towards others then you will not be striving with others. *They may strive with you* BUT *you will do everything in your power to maintain peace* with those around you. Bondservants loved not only their masters but all those who were in their master's household. If we are bondservants of Jesus then we will love other Christians simply because they belong to Christ. Matthew 10:24-25 says, *"A student is not above his teacher, nor a servant above his master. It is enough for the student to be like his teacher, and the servant like his master. If the head of the house has been called Beelzebub, how much more the members of his household!"*

I ask you, have you recognized that you are well with your Master now that you have been bought from the slavery of sin? If so, have you voluntarily committed your will to His? Do you love others in your Master's household because they belong to Him too?

I have seen women leave their husbands because they just didn't *feel* happy any more. Maybe their husband was going through a difficult season in life due to the loss of a job or perhaps a physical challenge. This is in contrast to taking on the attitude of a bondservant and it is exalting oneself above the happiness of the man they committed to love as well as above the needs of their children. Jesus was obedient to God. He was a bondservant. It cost Him his life. *His love, shown in His laying down His life for us, resulted in our salvation.* What might your love shown towards another, as you walk as a bond-servant, result in? Only God truly knows. As we develop a *servant's attitude by making Christ's attitude our attitude as **bondservants,*** we will know the satisfaction and the peace that results from putting others before ourselves no matter what others have done, are doing or will do.

I want to take a moment to address single women. Please ladies, if you are not married, do not let yourself fall into the trap of thinking that marriage will bring you fulfillment and satisfaction. The truth is that no human being, including a husband, can fill that void that exists in your soul. And to married women: you must not expect your husbands to fulfill and satisfy you. If you get married in order to have your needs met, you will surely be disappointed. Sometimes women say things like "if my husband would only talk to me more," or "if he would get home from work earlier, I would be happy. I would be satisfied." Again, the truth is that only God can fill the void you are experiencing.

Only God can bring genuine satisfaction. God is the One Who created that empty space and only He has the capacity to fill it. Once He fills that place He left empty, then you can experience an abundance of contentment. Then, the acceptance and pleasant emotions received from our husbands or from other people become the overflow in our lives. The fill up, however, can only come from God Himself. And we need filled up with Him daily!

We cannot depend on people to be the supply for the void in our lives and we cannot depend on people to meet our expectations. We are much less frustrated when we accept people the way God has made them and accept wherever they are in their walk with Him. In reality, they are out of our control anyway. Ultimately God is in control of the lives of those around us as well as our own life. He is also the One Who perfects us (Psalm 138:8). According to Word Wealth in The Spirit Filled Life Bible, this word perfect, *gamar*, refers to the completing, finishing, and perfecting of God's work in one's life.[7] God begins to work out His purposes in all of His children's lives and He does not stop until it is absolutely and completely complete.

A satisfied woman is a woman who allows God to be the One who fills the void in her life – not expecting people to do so. She is a woman who has a ***servant's heart and mind,*** *and* does not put her expectations on others. Instead, she puts other's needs above her own.

ROAD STOP:

Consider for a moment who in your life you depend on to make you happy.

What happens in your relationship when they fail to meet your expectations? Ask God to teach you to lean on and to look to Him for your happiness. Only He can satisfy.

CHAPTER NINE

What Defines Your Life?

"Then he said to them, "Watch out! Be on your guard against all kinds of greed; a man's life does not consist in the abundance of his possessions"
(Luke 12:15)

⬥

Another lure used to distract us so the enemy can attempt to prevent us from experiencing satisfaction is our desire for **things**. Our western society is definitely a materialistic society and material things are a popular substitute in the search for satisfaction. How many people do you know who are looking for satisfaction in *things*? You won't have to think long to think of someone whose life is defined by their possessions.

It amazes me, even as I look at those in the church, how the world's values have crept in. I see it all the time. One family purchases a new large screen TV. Then another family has to have one, but it has to be just a little bit better. A family purchases a new car. You see their friends driving a new one as well shortly thereafter. Never mind the budget. Never mind the needs of the children. Never mind about the bondage of debt that will keep them from doing the things God calls them to do. As we discussed in the early chapters of this book, we often call this "keeping up with the Joneses." With the initial purchase there is a sense of satisfaction, but a week later the sense of satisfaction is gone! A month later, you discover that you are no longer quite so impressed with your new purchase. The bills begin rolling in and your satisfaction disappears! Often, you begin contemplating what the next purchase will be while complaining about not having any "free" money.

Think about it. What would happen if a terrible storm came through and wiped out your home? What would happen to your sense of satisfaction if you were wiped out of material blessings? What a snare "**things**" can be! In Luke 12:15, we read, "Then he said to them, 'Watch out! Be on your guard against all kinds of greed; a man's life does not consist in the abundance of his possessions.'" In the Sermon on the Mount, Jesus warned people about laying up of treasures on the earth: earthly treasures cannot make us feel safe. Most people think that "*things*" will bring them satisfaction but in reality "*things*" can subtly **steal** from us the only satisfaction that really lasts. Our human tendency is to *pull away* from God as the value of our possessions increases. The more possessions we have, the more we tend to rely on *them* for security rather than upon *God*. This is why Jesus said in Matthew 19:24, "Again I tell you, it is easier for a camel to go through the eye of a **needle** than for a rich man to enter the kingdom of God." It is less likely for a wealthy man who has an accumulation of things to come to God. The rich man will tend to look at his riches and fail to recognize his need for God. Money and the things money purchases can easily become competition for the time and devotion that God desires for Himself alone.

A number of years ago, I had prospered as a small business owner. I was a single mother and God had given me the idea to open a communications company in order to provide for myself and my children. My husband had abandoned us and I was faced with a financial dilemma. Eventually I met Jon and he came to work with me. We made a great team and the business flourished. We eventually expanded from one to three store locations. At this time I thought of the business as my business since on faith and a shoestring I had done the ground work to get the business launched and the first store location opened. Getting those first customers is difficult and it takes a lot of perseverance not to quit before the harvest. Once there was a foundation of customers, business snowballed and subtly, my whole identity became wrapped up in being a successful business woman.

After a couple of years, Jon and I married and we thoroughly enjoyed working together in the busy communications business. Then one day God spoke to both of us in our individual prayer time to begin to prepare for ministry. We were already going to church four times a week. We were so hungry for Jesus, but the business was requiring more and more of our time and energy. One morning I awoke and God spoke to me to sell the business. I loved God, but to sell the business was asking a lot! It was my identity and besides, I had gone from barely surviving to thoroughly enjoying the fruit of my labor. Would God really require me to sacrifice the business and walk away from it? I was very much aware that God desired to be my identity. Yet my identity had become wrapped up in the business world as a woman who had made it against the odds – moving from a mother on food stamps and struggling to care for her children to owning a million dollar business with three store locations that helped and employed others! To sell the business was to lose my identity!

You see, "things" consist of more than material things. "Things" can be position, recognition, achievements, organizations, societies and even education. Although I knew God was the source and reason for my success, somehow this business had taken a place in my heart that should only belong to Him!

Of course, there were other things to consider as well — like my husband, my daughter and her husband and my son who were all employed in the business. After talking and praying with Jon, I was released to move ahead. I stepped out in faith and obedience in the midst of my fear and put the business up for sale. The business sold the first day it appeared in the trade journal! Thirty days later we were asking, "What next God?"

Although there have been challenges and even times when I could not see His hand, I have never regretted my obedience to Him in selling this business. Had I kept it, Jon and I would not have walked out the destiny God had planned for us – to plant and pastor a church as well as to begin a ministry designed to reach out to women in our community and beyond. Besides, my relationship with God was hindered due to the place the business had taken in my heart. Growing in relationship with Him and learning to walk by faith is the most awesome place to be! A growing, intimate relationship with our Father and Lord Jesus is the only thing any of us really need! This is what makes life work!

Material things strip us of our satisfaction when our identity becomes *wrapped* up in our *possessions.* We humanly think a man is defined by how much money he makes. We often hear people ask "how much is that man worth?" as if the worth of a man could be measured in dollars and cents. What nonsense! As Christians, we are defined by the value of the blood of Jesus. We are of infinite value even if we own nothing because of the infinite value of His life. The life of Jesus is what was paid for our eternal freedom, so Jesus must value us very greatly indeed!

The obsessive desire for *more things* has provoked innumerable get rich quick schemes and gambling opportunities. The prophet Jeremiah wrote in Jeremiah 17:11, *"Like a partridge that hatches eggs it did not lay is the man who gains riches by unjust means. When his life is half gone, they will desert him, and in the end he will prove to be a fool."* I have seen families destroyed because women fell for the deception that to be real women, they needed to go into the job market and "do something for themselves" by becoming successful in a profession. Some think they need a career to give their children all the "things" they desire, but the presence of their mother's love and guidance in their lives is the only thing these children are really in need of. All the other things are substitutes for the needed and desired relationship with mom.

Material things are temporary and do nothing to build the character of our children. Giving our children everything they desire prepares them to live out their lives searching for satisfaction in *things* that are temporary rather than in *relationship with Christ* which is eternal and the only true source of satisfaction. We need to accept that things are not going to fulfill us. Yet how many of us have acknowledged that truth in our minds, but we have not attempted to change our lifestyle or redirect our drive to acquire more and more.

Look at Elvis Presley, King of Rock and Roll. Few people in his time made as much money and acquired as much fame in as short a time as he did. It appeared that he had it all—money, airplanes, cars, mansions, fame, good looks and talent. Yet he died at age 42 on an overdose of pills after fighting serious bouts of depression. Things—they did not bring Elvis genuine satisfaction and they won't bring it to you either.

How about higher education? Higher education can be a thing that robs one of satisfaction if the degree becomes your identity. The key is to guard your heart from allowing **anything** to take God's place in your life and in your identity. Remember that He is the One who makes you who you are, not your degree or lack of degree. Education is good and can be used by God for the fulfillment of His purpose and plan for your life. Even secular colleges can be good as long as you know who God is and who you are. Without a solid foundation in the Word of God, though, I am afraid that much higher education is destroying our kids instead of helping them to fulfill the purpose God would desire for their lives. The statistics are staggering concerning the number of high school students who attend church before entering college but end up turning away from their belief in God. There are many professors in our schools and colleges who teach very convincingly against the reality of God. Therefore, we need to be sure to build a solid foundation in the lives of our children before they go to college, and we need to help them to prayerfully select the schools they will attend.

Take a look at the Apostle Paul. He was highly educated and had many advantages in his life. Yet he said that he counted all things as loss for the excellence of knowing Christ Jesus. It wasn't Paul's money, education, recognition, or profession that satisfied him. It was Jesus. There is nothing wrong with "things" in themselves. It is the danger of "things" becoming your goal that is the problem. For Paul, it was making Jesus Christ **the goal** of his life that brought him satisfaction. All else amounted to nothing in comparison. Philippians 3:10-15, *"I want to know Christ and the power of his resurrection and the fellowship of sharing in his sufferings, becoming like him in his death, and so, somehow, to attain to the* *resurrection from the dead. Not that I have already obtained all this, or have already been made perfect, but I press on to take hold of that for which Christ Jesus took hold of me. Brothers, I do not consider myself yet to have taken hold of it. But one thing I do: Forgetting what is behind and straining toward what is ahead, I press on toward the goal to win the prize for which God has called me heavenward in Christ Jesus. All of us who are mature should take such a view of things. And if on some point you think differently, that too God will make clear to you."*

Paul says he leaves the past behind. He has a mind focused on his goal of becoming like Christ. In the book of James we are told not to be double minded, meaning not to be undecided or vacillating. James tells us that the double-minded person is unstable in all his ways. Remember what Jesus said in Matthew 6:24, "No one can serve two masters. Either he will hate the one and love the other, or he will be devoted to the one and despise the other. You cannot serve both God and money." We must serve God with our whole heart. We cannot serve

God wholeheartedly and have acquiring riches as our goal at the same time.

What things are keeping you from Christ? What things are taking the place of true satisfaction in your life? To be satisfied women we need to have a *one-purpose mind*, setting our eyes on Jesus and Jesus alone. Being *double-minded*, being focused on acquiring riches as well as Jesus, will not lead you to a satisfied life.

How do we stay *one-purpose* minded? *We give our whole heart to Jesus alone and dedicate ourselves to doing all we can to be more and more like Him every day.* How do we do this? We **allocate** our *time* and our *things* according to how they will help us to achieve our goal which is to be like Christ. This is the way of a **one-purpose mind** and it leads to being a satisfied woman.

ROAD STOP:

At this juncture, ask God to show you where your focus has been. And remember, possessions are not evil in themselves. However, if things are your central focus, you should repent and turn your attention towards God. Allow Him to be first and He will take care of you.

CHAPTER TEN

Why Worry?

*"Do not be anxious about anything, but
in everything, by prayer and petition, with
thanksgiving, present your requests to God"
(Philippians 4:6)*

$\backsim\!\!\mathscr{S}\!\!\mathscr{S}\!\!\sim$

Another trap that can cause us to lose our satisfaction is *worry* or anxiety. God tells us to be
anxious for nothing but in everything let our requests
be made known unto God and the God of peace
shall keep our heart and mind (Philippians 4:6-7).
Worrying ensnares us and steals our sense of fulfillment and satisfaction. It tries to destroy our health
as well. We have all heard the story, "You don't get
ulcers from what you eat," said one doctor. "You get
ulcers from what is eating you."[8] "Those who are

extremely anxious," said John Calvin, himself prone to anxiety, "wear themselves out and become their own executioners."[9]

It is impossible to live as a satisfied woman if you are continually full of anxiety.

As we again look at Paul's life, we see that he had faced trials that, compared to ours, make our worst days seem like good ones. While in prison and faced with the possibility of execution, people were spreading dangerous rumors about him. Some of them even claimed to be Christians, but yet they were doing damage to Paul's reputation as a man of God. Some of their talk was even causing Paul to suffer even more persecution. Paul definitely had reason, humanly speaking, to be anxious. But Paul was not worried. Paul's attitude was: *"For me to live is Christ and to die is gain"* (Phil 1:21). He was ready to die in order to be with Christ; but he was willing to live on for the furtherance of the gospel and to help the Philippians in their spiritual journey. Why? – Because Paul was submitted to the will of God for his life. He had *surrendered his life* to Christ and understood that the *eternal plan and purpose of God was much greater* than his human mind was able to see or comprehend. Paul realized that no man or circumstance could take his life unless God allowed it. He understood God is sovereign, all powerful, all knowing, present with him at all times, and that God was working out *His* plan through the lives of those on earth, including his. Paul was satisfied in God's love and content to know that God was in control.

Paul's attitude of trust in the sovereignty of God reminds me of the account in Luke 19:10-11 when Christ stood in front of Pilate. Pilate said, "...don't you realize I have power either to free you or to crucify you?" Christ responded, "You would have no power over me if it were not given to you from above..."Paul understood this same truth of God's sovereign power over his life. No man had power over Paul's life, but only God. In other words, if God says "no" then it is not going to happen. If God says "stop" then it will stop. God is in control of all things. What peace indwells my soul as I meditate on God's sovereignty!

Paul exhorts the Philippians in Philippians 4:6, "Be anxious for nothing, but in everything by prayer and supplication, with thanksgiving, let your requests be made known to God;" and verse 7, "and the peace of God, which surpasses all understanding, will guard your hearts and minds through Christ Jesus." When we refuse to dwell on thoughts that are contrary to the attitudes we see in Paul and in Christ Himself, then our character and conduct will begin to line up with their character and conduct. Paul saw his *present circumstances* in light of the *future promises* of God. Therefore, he was able to transfer his burdens and concerns to Christ through earnest and extended prayer instead of worrying about them. The result was a life lived in God's ways and in God's peace. We can have God's supernatural peace in our lives, knowing that regardless of the concerns surrounding us, they are *momentary* when seen from the perspective of *eternity.*

It is good to set goals for our lives. But we must remember that our goals will be met only by the grace of God. Our days are held in His hands and only He knows what tomorrow holds. I see people worry about things that might happen in the future. Then, when that day comes, nothing happens. All is well. What a waste of energy and thought life! Matthew 6:34 tells us, "Therefore do not worry about tomorrow, for tomorrow will worry about itself. Each day has enough trouble of its own." We should shield our minds against worries about the days ahead if we want to be content today.

What are the concerns you have *today*? Whether it is paying the bills, raising your children, making a decision about a company move and promotion, your health or the health of a loved one, "Seek the kingdom of God, and all these things shall be added to you" (Luke 12:31 NKJV). God tells us to look to Him, take care of His business and He will take care of ours. My husband often comments on this saying, "What a great deal!"

To live as a satisfied woman requires that I live with a **shielded mind**—one that stays focused on God and His Kingdom. I can guard my mind by praying before I do anything. I can release my fears and worries to Him. I can make changes if changes are needed. For instance, if I am fretting over the bills, I might want to implement a change in our family budget and lifestyle. If I am concerned about my health because I am dealing with high blood pressure, then I might want to make an appointment with the doctor and begin to change my eating and exercise habits. Taking some steps to improve the particular area of life that is giving you concern can help bridge the gap between worrying and faith.

I can shield my mind by making a "worry list" and taking it daily to the Lord, transferring my burdens to Christ. No matter what, I give thanks to Him. I look to Him as my tower of refuge and strength and the sovereign, all-powerful God. I can guard my mind from thoughts that are contrary to the Word of God. I can take my thoughts captive to the obedience of Christ (2 Cor. 10:5) and insist on thinking thoughts that are true, noble, right, pure, lovely, admirable, excellent and praiseworthy (Philippians 4:8).

I can guard my mind as I set my thoughts on Jesus, and the riches I have in Him. Philippians 4:19 tells me "...my God will meet all (my) needs according to his glorious riches in Christ Jesus." If I know that God will meet all my needs, then why worry? Worry is a small trickle of fear that twists and turns through the mind until it cuts a channel into which all other thoughts are drained. "Worry is a form of atheism, for it betrays a lack of faith and trust in God" (Attributed to Bishop Fulton J. Sheen) [10]

To close this chapter I want to share a story. It goes like this:

"I have a mountain of credit card debt," one man told another. "I've lost my job, my car is being repossessed, and our house is in foreclosure, but I'm not worried.

"Not worried about it!" exclaimed his friend.

"No. I've hired a professional worrier. He does all my worrying for me, and that way I don't have to think about it."

"That's fantastic. How much does your professional worrier charge for his services?"

"Fifty thousand dollars a year," replied the first man.

"Fifty thousand dollars a year!" "Where are you going to get that kind of money?"

"I don't know, came the reply. "That's his worry!"

In a sense, the Lord's servants do have a professional worrier to do all our worrying for us. As 1 Peter 5:7 says, "You can throw the whole weight of your anxieties upon him, for you are his personal concern" (Phillips).[11]

ROAD STOP:

What do you do when worry arises? Do you immediately turn to God for His wisdom to handle your concerns? If not, make a decision today and begin to diligently set your mind to change the habits you have formed. Begin by going first to God with everything that concerns you.

Have you allowed your life to get out of control by focusing on situations of worry MORE THAN other business of life? If so, you should realize that worry is a sin against God. Worry is a product of fear which springs from the absence of God's love being perfected in us. Fear is the opposite of love. "There is *no* fear in love, 1 John 4:18." And love activates faith. For [if we are] in Christ Jesus, neither circumcision nor uncircumcision counts for anything, but only faith **activated** and energized and expressed and working through love" (Galatians 5:6 AMP). Hebrews 11:6 says, "And without faith it is impossible to please God, because anyone who comes to him must believe that he exists and that he rewards those who earnestly seek him".

Confess your lack of trust in God as sin, ask for forgiveness and ask Him to help you to develop new behavior patterns to implement change in your lifestyle. Ask Him to show you how to trust Him.

CHAPTER ELEVEN
An Introduction to the Beatitudes

Happiness

"Blessed or Happy is the man who..."

◁◯▷

We have been talking about "contentment" or "satisfaction" as one of two ingredients found in 1Timothy 6:6: "But godliness with *contentment* is great gain." Now that you have learned to cultivate the "mind of Christ" for *your* mind, we need to look at the other ingredient found in 1 Timothy 6:6 that is needed for an abundant, fulfilled and satisfied life. That ingredient is **"godliness"**. I Timothy 6:6 emphasizes to us the importance of *our attitude towards God*. According to Vines Dictionary, godliness "denotes that piety which, characterized by a

God ward attitude, does that which is well-pleasing to Him."[12] When you have a reverence towards God, it will show itself in your walk with God in what you *choose **to do*** or *choose **not** to do* due to your reverence and fear of God. In other words, without a lifestyle or walk that reflects piety and devotion towards God, you will not be content and you will not truly experience the abundant life that is available to you.

We are now going to look in Matthew 5 for some insight to what our actions or walk with God might look like when we are ruled according to our reverence for God. When we look at the beatitudes in Matthew 5:3-12, we discover that the first word in each of the beatitudes is *"blessed"*. The amplified Bible describes the word "blessed" as "happy, to be envied, and spiritually prosperous—with life-joy and satisfaction in God's favor and salvation, regardless of the outward conditions." We can see then that happiness is a *result* of a life lived for Christ. Blessedness is not available from the world or any human resource. It is not circumstantial, tangible and emotional. It is divine, deep, lasting and accessible.

Blessedness comes from walking with God. So the eight qualities described in the beatitudes give us descriptions of *how we are to live* in order to experience this type of *happiness* in our lives.

Some of the early movies made about the life of Jesus presented Him as a man who was austere and who saw life as no laughing matter. It is as if the producers of those movies thought that seriousness is the definition of godliness. I was so thrilled when the newer versions were made and we were shown a smiling Jesus. In these movies, Jesus is depicted as full of joy as He lived His life on earth serving, preaching, teaching and healing. This is much closer to what we read in the bible. Jesus indeed had his trials and challenges, yet He was content in being in the Center of God's plan and purpose for His life. He was blessed because He was God-centered in all that He thought, said and did due to His reverence for God.

Looking at the Beatitudes in Matthew chapter five, we see *the* abundance available to the woman who is content living life through her *reverence towards God which is reflected in her walk with*

God. Each one of the eight beatitudes begins with the word "blessed". In the next six chapters we will take a closer look at developing these eight qualities in our lives that we may experience the *blessed life* as described in the beatitudes – a life that is "happy, to be envied, and spiritually prosperous—with life-joy and *satisfaction* in God's favor and salvation, regardless of the outward conditions."

ROAD STOP:

How did you describe godliness before reading this chapter? Does your lifestyle reflect a reverence *for* or *against* God?

CHAPTER TWELVE

The Poor in Spirit

*"God blesses those who realize their need for him,
for the Kingdom of Heaven is given to them"
(Matthew 5:3 NLT)*

❦

"Blessed (happy, to be envied, and spiritually prosperous – with life-joy and satisfaction in God's favor and salvation, regardless of their outward conditions) are the poor in spirit (the humble, who rate themselves insignificant), for theirs is the kingdom of heaven!" (Matthew 5:3 AMP)

The woman who is "poor in spirit" is the one whose soul contains less of her and more of God. You might picture this person as being at the end of their rope. Without more rope to hold onto, they now take hold of God. They realize their need for Him and reach out for Him with desperate eagerness.

Being spiritually poor is recognizing that we are totally dependent on God and His grace. No one begins their walk with God by working for the privilege and no one finishes their walk by earning it. We are to continually draw our worth from Jesus. There is NOTHING we can do to earn a relationship with Jesus. There is nothing we can do to deserve His blessing on our lives. Even so, when we are weak, He is strong. We become poor in spirit when we recognize that anything of value that we are is because of the grace of God. God alone gets all the glory!

The word humble comes from the root word humus, which is ground. It is defined as:

1. Marked by meekness or modesty in behavior, attitude, or spirit; not arrogant or prideful.

2. Showing deferential or submissive respect: *a humble apology.*

3. Low in rank, quality, or station; unpretentious or lowly: *a humble cottage.* [13]

One who is humble is like the ground which is composed of clay. God is the Potter and we are but the clay. He can shape us into whatever vessel He desires and He can reshape us at any time. A woman who is poor in spirit is one who is putting her trust in God and not in her degrees, positions, abilities, etc. She realizes and accepts that it is God who decides who will be promoted and who will be demoted.

Hudson Taylor, explaining his success said, "I think God was looking for a little man, little enough so that He could show Himself strong through him. A man can receive nothing, except it be given him from heaven."[14] Without Him, we are nothing and in control of nothing. He is our every thing! He is our all in all! If it were not for the grace of God, how would I go? Being poor in spirit is living as a *surrendered vessel* to God, allowing Christ to work through us for His purposes and realizing that all glory belongs to Him. As a student, Jonathan Blanchard, who later would establish both Wheaton and Knox Colleges, prayed this simple prayer: "O my Savior God, deliver me from sluggishness on the one hand and from ambition on the other. May I do all I can do, and feel no more lifted up than if I did nothing."[15]

As women of God, we can do everything God calls us to do because it is the power and wisdom of God that works through us to accomplish His will. When we begin stepping out in faith and seeing the hand of God move through us, we must guard against pride. To quote my husband, "The truth is this — pride must die in you so God can work through you."[16] It is imperative to remember that it is God who is accomplishing great things for *His* glory. It is not our talent or ability that is succeeding. Therefore, to God is all the glory in and for all things! Once when an acquaintance praised Johann Sebastian Bach for his wonderful skill as an organist, he replied with characteristic humility and wit: "There is nothing very wonderful about it. You have only to hit the right notes at the right moment and the instrument does the rest."[17]

As one who is poor in spirit, you recognize and acknowledge your spiritual need and you depend on God alone rather than on your own goodness. Again, my husband quoting William Barclay, put it like this in a recent sermon on humility, "Blessed is the man who has realized his own utter helplessness, and who has put his whole trust in God. When a man has realized his own utter helplessness and has put his whole trust in God, there will enter into his life two things which are opposite sides of the same thing. He will become completely detached from things, for he will know that things have not got it in them to bring *happiness or security*; and he will become completely attached to God, for he will know that *God alone* can bring him help, and hope, and strength. The man who is poor in spirit is the man who has realized that things mean nothing, and that God means everything." [18]

The poor in spirit have *no exaggerated* sense of importance. I think this poem by John Oxenham describes the poor in spirit well:

Is your place a small place?
Tend it with care! –
He set you there.

Is your place a large place?
Guard it with care! –
He set you there.

What're your place, it is
Not yours alone, but His
Who set you there.[19]

As we believe we are blessed in our spiritual poverty, we also need to believe the second half of this beatitude. Right now today, we possess the kingdom of heaven. *We can enjoy the promise of happiness today!* Son-ship, righteousness, comfort, fullness, mercy, peace and great reward belong to us **NOW** in our life upon earth.

ROAD STOP:

Think about your life for a moment. Does your life show that you are poor in spirit? Are you demonstrating humility of mind? Are you authentic in your relationships? Do you have a joyful countenance because of your confidence in God? Do you realize that things mean nothing and God means everything? These are characteristics of a woman who walks with God as a satisfied woman.

CHAPTER THIRTEEN

Happy Are Those Who Mourn

"Blessed Are Those Who Mourn. God blesses those who mourn, for they will be comforted"
(Matthew 5:4 NLT)

B lessed or happy are those who mourn. When you have lost what is most dear to you, then you are really *able to embrace God.* There are many different kinds of mourning in this life. I am going to focus on one kind of mourning, one which the Bible equates with repentance. When we think about the fact that every time we sin we are sinning against God Himself, the seriousness of our sin becomes evident to us. Awareness of the seriousness of our sin causes us to mourn over whatever we have done that displeases God. *As we give up our sin* and *mourn over it*, we experience forgiveness from God and our contentment is renewed. A woman who is walking with God mourns over the realization that she has been sinning against God and she mourns over the affect that sin has on her fellowship with Him.

Had it not been for the fall of man, we would be ruling with God and reflecting the glory of God in our lives. We would have an unhindered, intimate relationship with God. But, because of the sin of Adam and Eve, we have inherited a human nature that is dominated by sin, depraved and desecrates everything we touch.

The Bible, when it talks about sin is not telling us to walk around with our head hung low and a frown on our faces. We have great things to celebrate in Christ Jesus, and number one on the celebration list is forgiveness! However, when we understand the gravity of our sin, we cannot do anything else but mourn our broken relationship with God, and thank God for the blood of Jesus that restores us! The Heidelberg Catechism expresses it: *(LORD'S DAY!)

1. What is your only comfort in life and in death?
   That I am not my own but belong to my
   faithful Savior Jesus Christ.

2. What must you know to live and die in the joy
   of this comfort?
   Three things: first, how great my sin and
   misery are; second, how I am set free from all
   my sins and misery; third, how I am to thank
   God for such deliverance."

How can we experience happiness and satisfaction at the same time that we are sad and mourning over our sin? Happiness and satisfaction are *spiritual* elements not *circumstantial or emotional*. We should not wipe away the thoughts of our sin too quickly but instead *give the conviction of sin a chance to grow into true repentance*. Mourning is the outgrowth of true desperation and brokenness for your sin. Think about Job's outlook on his sin: "I despise myself and repent in dust and ashes" (Job 42:6). Consider Peter in Matthew 26:75 who after denying he knew Jesus "wept bitterly" , and David after recognizing his sin in taking another man's wife said, "*Against you, you only, have I sinned and done what is evil in your sight, so that you are proved right when you speak and justified when you judge*"(Psalm 51:4). When we mourn over our sin, we will begin to experience repentance. Repentance is turning away from our sin and facing toward God. The Bible promises that when we repent God forgives us and cleanses us from the effects of the sin in our lives (I John 1:9). As we experience God's forgiveness, we begin to experience that freedom, satisfaction and happiness we have come to expect in our relationship with Jesus (Isaiah 57:15).

In Matthew 5:4, God promises to comfort those who mourn. We have talked primarily about mourning over sin and have learned that the woman who mourns over h*er own sin* will experience repentance and forgiveness from God. All obstacles to her relationship with God will be removed so that she can enjoy the fruits of that relationship in her life. God will comfort her by removing the effects of her sin in her life and restoring her contentment and satisfaction in Him.

Just as a side note, I want to explain that I don't think all grief comes from letting someone or something take the place of God in our lives. There are times we grieve the loss of a mate, a child or a parent. Mourning can be the unavoidable and inevitable consequence of loving while we are in this life. I think this is the reason God makes such a bold promise to us here. He does not want us to withdraw our love from people in spite of the fact that loving will inevitably bring pain. He doesn't promise to take away the pain but He does promise to comfort us in it. And His comfort is not like the sympathy we get from people but rather the very nature of the Holy Spirit Himself Who calls Himself the Comforter. If you find yourself in a time of grieving the loss of a loved one, please know that the Holy Spirit is with you and He will hold your hand through what we call the "grieving process." It is a process and it takes time to heal our losses to death. I believe it is so difficult for us because we were created as eternal beings, to live forever. Our emotions were not created to handle death. But God has sent the Holy

Spirit to comfort you and you can know that He will bring you through to the place where you will be able to enjoy the good memories without the pain of the absence. Meanwhile, hold on to the promise we have in Him of eternal life. You will see your loved one again! *"Weeping may last for the night, but a shout of joy comes in the morning" (Psalm 30:5b).*

ROAD STOP:

When you confess your sin, do you do it casually and expect God to forgive you and cleanse you? Or do you think about the gravity of your sin and allow the conviction to bring you to a place of TRUE REPENTANCE?

As everything is received in the Christian faith, forgiveness is received by faith and not by sight. There is only one thing worse than sin and that is to *deny* our sin. Take time and truly repent. Then receive by faith the promise of 1 John 1:9, *"He cleanses us from all unrighteousness,"* and you will live as a blessed and highly favored woman.

CHAPTER FOURTEEN

Meekness Leads to Rest

"God blesses those who are gentle and lowly,
for the whole earth will belong to them"
(Matthew 5:5 NLT)

◁━━▷

In verse 5 of Matthew chapter 5, God tells us that the one who is "Blessed (happy, blithesome, joyous, spiritually prosperous—with life-joy and satisfaction in God's favor and salvation, regardless of their outward conditions) are the meek (the mild, patient, long-suffering), for they shall inherit the earth! (AMP) These blessed people are those who walk in meekness and are patient. They are at peace with God about the way He made them. The Message Bible puts it like this, "You're blessed when you're content with just who you are—no more, no less. That's the moment you find yourselves proud owners of everything that can't be bought."

A.W. Tozer describes meekness in his book, "The Pursuit of God. "Jesus *calls us* to *His rest*, and *meekness* is *His method*. The meek man cares not at all who is greater than he, for he has long ago decided that the esteem of the world is not worth the effort. The rest Christ offers is the rest of meekness, the blessed relief which comes when **we accept ourselves** for **what we are** and **cease to pretend**. It will take some courage at first, but the needed grace will come as we learn that we are sharing in this new and easy yoke with the strong Son of God Himself."[20] (Emphasis mine)

The esteem of the world will come and go. Because the world's opinion is fickle and unreliable, only a very foolish woman will put her trust there. Besides, no one in the world has a value higher than the Son of God, so receive your esteem from Him. The praise of people will always disappoint you.

Meekness does not connote *weakness*, but rather *controlled strength*. I have heard my husband use "meekness" to describe a wild stallion that has been tamed and bridled to the point that he now yields to being ridden. That stallion still has all the strength it had when it was wild, but his strength is now under control. The stallion has surrendered his strength to his master's direction.

Meekness and humility are interwoven throughout Scripture. We see examples of these character traits in the lives of the Apostle Paul, Jesus and King David. Paul's meekness is seen in the way he assesses himself in regarding others more highly than himself. Note the progression of his growth in meekness in his choice of comparison. In 1 Corinthians 15:9 he states that he is the least of all *apostles* – "For I am the least of the apostles and do not even deserve to be called an apostle, because I persecuted the church of God." Then he says in Ephesians 3:8 that he is the least of all the *saints* – "Although I am less than the least of all God's people, this grace was given me: to preach to the Gentiles the unsearchable riches of Christ." His last assessment was that he is the chief of *sinners* in 1 Timothy 1:15 – "Here is a trustworthy saying that deserves full acceptance: Christ Jesus came into the world to save sinners—of whom I am the worst."

Jesus, of course, is the greatest example of all. Humility and meekness are exhibited through His willingness to leave heaven and come to earth as a man. He does not exalt Himself as God and DELIVER Himself from the plan and purpose of God, but willingly SUBMITS to the cross in order that you and I could be saved and reconciled to God. No man has ever or ever will exhibit such love for others, putting others before themselves and laying their life down that others might live, as Christ Jesus has done. The example of His humility and meekness is summed up in Philippians 2:1-8,

> *"If you have any encouragement from being united with Christ, if any comfort from his love, if any fellowship with the Spirit, if any tenderness and compassion, then make my joy complete by being like-minded, having the same love, being one in spirit and purpose. Do nothing out of selfish ambition or vain*

conceit, but in humility consider others better than yourselves. Each of you should look not only to your own interests, but also to the interests of others. Your attitude should be the same as that of Christ Jesus: Who, being in very nature God, did not consider equality with God something to be grasped, but made himself nothing, taking the very nature of a servant, being made in human likeness. And being found in appearance as a man, he humbled himself and became obedient to death— even death on a cross!"

Power and strength under control as well as the willingness to submit to God's will and put others above oneself can be seen in one who is meek. This is most evident in the life of Christ.

We see Abraham, while he was still called Abram, exhibiting the quality of meekness in Genesis 13. Lot, Abram's nephew was traveling with Abram and both had a great number of possessions in flocks, herds and tents – so great that the land could not support them. Quarrels arose between Lot's herdsmen and Abram's herdsmen. Abram desiring to keep peace between himself and Lot suggested that there was plenty of land for the two to choose from so why not part company. We see Abram's meekness displayed as he allows Lot to choose the best land, the Jordan Valley where the land was well watered and green. Abram gave up his right to choose first and took the land that appeared second best. Are you beginning to understand the spiritual quality called meekness?

Let us look at another example of meekness. We see Moses being challenged in Numbers 11-12. The people began complaining about their hardships and expecting Moses to do something about it. Then the riffraff (as the Message Bible calls them) among the people began craving meat and soon had the people of Israel complaining. Moses heard the whining of the people continuously. Next Moses' brother Aaron and his sister Miriam began talking about Moses behind his back. They questioned his decision to marry a Cushite woman and they questioned his spiritual leadership saying, "Is it only through Moses that God speaks? Doesn't he also speak through us?" (Numbers 12:4 MSG) God heard this, called the three of them together, their attitudes were revealed to Moses' and God's judgment fell on Miriam in the form of leprosy. Through all of this, Moses remained meek, and *did not become defensive.* "Aaron said to Moses, 'Please, my master, please don't come down so hard on us for this foolish and thoughtless sin. Please don't make her like a stillborn baby coming out of its mother's womb with half its body decomposed.' And Moses prayed to GOD: Please, God, heal her, please heal her" (Numbers 12:11-13 MSG). Would you remain so meek in a situation like this? I admit I need to continue growing in this area. How about you? What areas do you find it difficult to exhibit meekness?

Then there are the "3:16" verses where meekness and humility are so clearly demonstrated:

- John 3:16, *"For God so loved the world that he gave his one and only Son, that*

whoever believes in him shall not perish
but have eternal life"

- 1 John 3:16,*"This is how we know what
  love is: Jesus Christ laid down his life for
  us. And we ought to lay down our lives for
  our brothers"*

- Colossians 3:16,*"Let the word of Christ
  dwell in you richly as you teach and
  admonish one another with all wisdom,
  and as you sing psalms, hymns and spiritual songs with gratitude in your hearts
  to God. "*

Meekness is an **attitude** of *humility* and *submission* to God. Those who are meek continually look to
God to give them life and blessings and will therefore inherit the land. This is in contrast to those who
live separated from God and attempt to take posses-
sion of the land and wealth by evil means instead of
looking to and trusting in God. Do you know what I
mean by evil means? You may be surprised to know
that a*ny means that does not include God is evil.*

There is a place of rest that God has for those who are meek, a place where all striving ceases and a child of God surrenders to the will and purpose of God. A woman who has learned meekness *can follow, she can go last, she can be transparent,* and she can *recall her vulnerabilities* without feeling threatened or defensive. *A meek woman regards others more highly than herself; she renounces her rights instead of fighting for them, and she is not easily offended.*

I love this quote from A.W. Tozer in The Pursuit of God. It speaks to a common misunderstanding concerning meekness:

"The meek man is not a human mouse afflicted with a sense of his own inferiority. Rather, he may be in his moral life as bold as a lion and as strong as Samson; but he has stopped being fooled about himself. He has accepted God's estimate of his own life. He knows he is as weak and helpless as God has declared him to be, but paradoxically, he knows at the same time that he is, in the sight of God, more important than angels...He knows

well that the world will never see him as God sees him, and he has stopped caring."[21]

Mr. Tozer understood that godly meekness is not the same thing as feelings of inferiority. True meekness and humility do not come from a lack of confidence or a lack of boldness. The meek woman is not a human mouse afflicted with a sense of inferiority. She is a woman of God who knows and accepts that the world will never see her as God sees her. *But she no longer cares.* She finds her **adequacy** and **fulfillment** in God alone.

To walk in meekness, I suggest that you pray Psalm 17:14, *"O LORD, by your hand save me from such men, from men of this world whose reward is in this life…"* A woman who cultivates meekness in her life will be at peace in her soul. She will be exalted by God and walk in His favor.

ROAD STOP:

To examine your life for meekness, ask yourself these five questions. Are you content with whom you are, no more and no less? Are you quick to listen and slow to speak (James 1:19), putting a guard over your mouth? *It is out of the heart that the mouth speaks (Matthew 12:34), your words testify to your meekness or lack of it.* Are you operating as a bond servant, loving Christ as your Master and serving in His household, the church? *If you are operating as a bond servant, then you will have **no** problem with being treated like a servant.* Are you happy when others are successful and receive affirmation even when you do not? Do you always have to be first?

CHAPTER FIFTEEN

Hunger and Thirst for Right Standing

"Blessed are those who hunger and thirst for righteousness, for they will be filled"
(Matthew 5:6 NIV)

⤳

The Amplified Bible composes the above verse, "Blessed and fortunate and happy and spiritually prosperous (in that state in which the born-again child of God enjoys His favor and salvation) are those who hunger and thirst for righteousness (uprightness and right standing with God), for they shall be completely satisfied."

Righteousness is a *legal term* in the Bible. This verse tells us that, legally, we have right standing with God because Christ exchanged places with us.

Jesus took our deserved place on the cross and gave us His righteousness which we did not merit. We are now clothed in the righteousness of Christ Jesus.

Righteousness is also a relational term in the Bible in that it describes the relationship between a born-again Christian and God. Being in a state of righteousness is being right in your relationship with God and others and living your life in a way that agrees with God.

Soul satisfaction does not come from things that can be acquired in the world. Although we do have physical needs that must be met, true soul satisfaction does not come from simply having our physical needs met. True soul satisfaction comes when our hunger for spiritual things – the things of God – is fulfilled. Matthew 6:33 tells us to seek first the kingdom of God and His righteousness and then all these other things – the natural, physical needs we all have – will be added to us. In other words, when we take care of God's business, then He will take care of ours. It is not that the pursuit of other things is wrong in itself. Their pursuit is wrong when it doesn't *flow out from* the primary pursuit of God. It is wrong when it isn't a *result* of our pursuing God first.

If you don't know where you are going, you will wind up somewhere else. So, **set your mind on the things of God first and foremost.** Paul charged the Christians in Colossians 3:2 "*set your mind on things above.*" Then he challenged them to "*put on*" godly virtues, by which he meant to live *godly lives.* Hungering for righteousness is *having a desire to have life God's way!* It is seeking God's uprightness and justice rather than having confidence in our selves and our own goodness.

Do you remember the movie, <u>Attack of the Clones</u>? Anakin Skywalker becomes attached to things and becomes the evil Darth Vader. He is unable to let go of his mother and his girlfriend. Becoming attached to things makes you greedy. You are greedy when you fear you are going to lose things. That fear leads you to the dark side when you begin to search for the power to keep hold of things. Those who hunger for righteousness are just the opposite. They are not attached to things. They have discovered that life is empty and has no meaning without God. In Romans 6:21-22 Paul admonishes the Christians in Rome, *"What benefit did you reap at that time from the things you are now ashamed of? Those things result in death! But now that you have been set free from sin and have become slaves to God the benefit you reap leads to holiness and the result is eternal life".*

As satisfied women we are continually hungering to see God's ways at work in our lives and in our world. As Christians, we are continually growing in His ways. His name is like honey on our lips and His spirit is water to our soul. As we hunger and thirst for God, He satisfies our hunger with the richest of spiritual food. He satisfies us with His very Presence and we say, "I am a satisfied woman". Yet I desire more of Him today than yesterday because I see that there is more of Him that I have not yet experienced.

ROAD STOP:

Do you have a hunger and thirst for God, desiring to know Him and His ways more intimately? God tells us in Proverbs 8:17, *"I love those who love me, and those who seek me find me."* You can go to Him by faith and ask Him to give you a love for Him and He will do it.

> *"This is the confidence we have in approaching God: that if we ask anything according to his will, he hears us"*
>
> (1 John 5:14).

Luke 10:27, *"'Love the Lord your God with all your heart and with all your soul and with all your strength and with all your mind'; and, 'Love your neighbor as yourself.'"*

Do you love Him with all your heart, soul, strength and mind? Ask Him to give you this kind of love for Him! James 4:2b tells us we have not because we ask not.

> *"May the Lord direct your hearts into God's love and Christ's perseverance"*
>
> (2 Thess. 3:5).

CHAPTER SIXTEEN

The One Who Cares is Cared For

"You're blessed when you care.
At the moment of being 'care full,'
you find yourselves 'cared for'"
(Matt 5:7 The Message Bible)

❧

In verse 7 of Matthew Chapter 5, we see that the one who is "Blessed (*happy, to be envied, and spiritually prosperous—with life-joy and satisfaction in God's favor and salvation, regardless of the outward conditions) are the merciful for they shall obtain mercy!*" is the one who cares. As you show mercy you receive mercy. The Message Bible states that "as you are *care full* (that is, full of care for others), you find yourself *cared for* by God".

I am reminded of the following story: A young lady who occasionally walked through the park after work, stopped one day to have her picture taken by a photographer. She was very excited about her picture being taken. As she walked out of the park, she looked at the Polaroid picture in total amazement. She turned and headed back to the photographer. When she got there, she said, "This is not right! This is not right! You have not done me justice!" The photographer looked at the picture and looked at her and stated, "Miss, you don't need justice, what you need is mercy."[22]

On a more serious note...As I have heard our pastor, Michael Fletcher, say so many times, "We do not want God to deal with us justly. What we want is mercy!" If God dealt with us justly, none of us would be here today. Sometimes we think we look pretty good, but if we stop and really look into our hearts where God is checking us out, justice is not what we want. The following story gives us a good description of mercy:

A mother once approached Napoleon seeking a pardon for her son. The emperor replied that the young man had committed a certain offense twice and justice demanded death.

"But I don't ask for justice," the mother explained. "I plead for mercy."

"But your son does not deserve mercy," Napoleon replied.

"Sir," the woman cried, "it would not be mercy if he deserved it, and mercy is all I ask for."

"Well, then," the emperor said, "I will have mercy." And he spared the woman's son."[23]

When you are walking in mercy toward another, you do more than pray for them; you begin *to walk in that person's shoes*, empathizing with their experience. You ask questions because you want to understand what they are experiencing so you can help in some way. "Do you know why your spouse is doing those things?" you may ask your friend. "Do you know the root cause of their behavior, addiction, etc.?" you want to know. Recognizing your own weaknesses and sin nature, you are able to deal gently with those who are lacking knowledge or are going astray. Just as we need and expect so much mercy from God and others, so we must be willing to show mercy to others.

Scripture tells us that Jesus was a man of sorrows. Hebrews 4:15 says, "For we do not have a high priest who is unable to sympathize with our weaknesses, but we have one who has been tempted in every way, just as we are—yet was without sin". I am so glad that Jesus did not leave me in my sin! Jesus understands and extends His mercy to me. He walks with me through my troubles and He wants me to walk through troubles alongside others. He wants me to give support and encouragement to those who are struggling and allow the Holy Spirit to mend and heal the brokenhearted in His way and in His timing.

"Judgment without mercy will be shown to anyone who has not been merciful. Mercy triumphs over judgment!" (James 2:13). Martin Luther said, "What is it to serve God and to do His will? Nothing else than to show mercy to our neighbor. For it is our neighbor who needs our service; God in heaven needs it not".[24] Spiritual healthiness is being able to walk in God's Presence and enjoy Him ourselves, yet still feel the hurts of people around us who do not know Him. As you walk in mercy toward others, you receive mercy from our heavenly Father, and you are enabled to live as a satisfied woman.

ROAD STOP:

Are you quick to judge others? Or are you walking in love, showing mercy toward others as mercy has been shown towards you by our Father? If you have been one who judges instead of being merciful, repent of this sin and begin showing mercy towards others. Remember, only God can be the judge. He intricately formed each of us in our mother's womb, even the sinner you are judging! Only God knows the road they have traveled and how their life experiences have affected them. He knows every place that needs healing, every place that needs repentance, and He alone can shepherd them into a place of wholeness and righteousness.

Sometimes people who withhold mercy from others or who have a tendency towards walking with a judgmental attitude have not themselves accepted the completed work of Christ at Calvary. Remember, if not but for the grace of God, how is it YOU would go? If you tend to be judgmental towards others, you may be walking in the deception that "those who fail are unloveable and deserve to be criticized and condemned." If so, you are probably suffering from low self worth and may be withdrawing from God. Christ was the sacrifice for your sins as well as for that individual whom you are setting blame upon. His substitutionary death on the cross paid the penalty of your sin and hers and He has given you both His righteousness. With His righteousness now being hers, how can you judge her and how can you judge yourself?

Memorize and ask God to imprint the Truth of Ephesians 2:4-5 into your mind and soul, *"But because of his great love for us, God, who is rich in mercy, made us alive with Christ even when we were dead in transgressions—it is by grace you have been saved."*

CHAPTER SEVENTEEN

Cultivating a Passion for Purity

"God blesses those whose hearts are pure,
for they will see God"
(Matthew 5:8 NLV)

〜♒〜

Wouldn't you love to see God's will dominant in your choices, your thoughts, your actions, and your motives? Guess what? Matthew 5:8 promises us that, if we permit the Spirit of God to purify our hearts then we will see God working through us in all areas of our life. It is God who began a good work in you and He will carry it to completion (Philippians 1:6). Our job is to set our eyes on Him and *cooperate*. How do we cooperate?

First of all, we pray regularly. Psalm 19:12-13 cries out to God,

> *"Who can discern his errors?*
> *Forgive my hidden faults.*
> *Keep your servant also from willful sins;*
> *may they not rule over me.*
> *Then will I be blameless,*
> *innocent of great transgression."*

Secondly, we need to guard our hearts. Proverbs 4:23 reads, *"Above all else, guard your heart, for it is the wellspring of life."* We need to guard what we allow to enter into our hearts through the gateway of our eyes and our ears. Be particular about what you choose to *look at* and what you choose to *listen to.*

Another way to cooperate with God is to read Scripture and allow the Word to get in your heart. *"Do not let this Book of the Law depart from your mouth; meditate on it day and night, so that you may be careful to do everything written in it. Then you will be prosperous and successful"* (Joshua 1:8). Meditating is more than a quick reading and checking another item off your list for the day. According to J. I. Packer, meditating has to do with turning your knowledge *about* God into a knowledge *of* God. In his book, <u>Knowing God</u>, Packer states, "Meditation is the activity of calling to mind, and thinking over, and dwelling on, and applying to oneself, the various things that one knows about the works and ways and purposes and promises of God." He further says, "It's purpose is to clear one's mental and spiritual vision of God, and to let his truth make its full and proper impact on one's mind and heart."[25]

A fourth way to cooperate with God is to speak to your self. But be careful— human tendency is to listen to your self rather than talk to your self. Follow the example David gives us in Psalm 42:5, 11, "Why are you downcast, O my soul? Why so disturbed within me? Put your hope in God, for I will yet praise him, my Savior and my God." We need to encourage ourselves and even *command* ourselves to obey God the way David did.

A fifth method of cooperating with God is to train your mind to think about Jesus, refusing to give place to any thought that comes your way that is not godly.

I determined a number of years ago that I wanted God to be my first thought each morning. I asked God to help me. To help me to cooperate with Him as He helps me, I speak to Him and tell Him good night before I go to bed. When I first open my eyes in the morning, I immediately say "Good morning, Father. Thank you for this day. You have made it and I will rejoice and be glad in it." I have found this to be a great way to train my mind to think upon Jesus throughout the day. You can *choose* to consciously and intentionally begin your day with Him.

What do you do when ungodly thoughts enter your mind? The mind is often where the "war of the thoughts" takes place. How can you win this war? One important weapon against evil thoughts is to learn how to produce a counter-thought. A counter-thought is a powerful thought that provokes an image in the mind that opposes the evil thought. The more powerful the ungodly image or thought, the more powerful the counter-image must be to counteract the unwanted image.

If you have an area that you struggle with continuously, I suggest you find Scriptures that you can use to replace those unwanted thoughts. For instance, if you struggle with judgmental thoughts, then you might develop a set of 3" x 5" index cards on which you write scripture and references that will serve as counter-thoughts for those thoughts of judgment towards another or towards yourself whichever the case may be. Perhaps you will even want two sets of scriptures – one set to remind you of your own sin and the judgment you deserved but did not receive from Jesus; and another set to remind you of the awesome fact that God Himself has not judged you but has shown mercy towards you. It is also a good idea to develop a mind picture to go along with these Scriptures. Pictures speak powerfully to our minds and, when coupled with the Word of God, pictures will help you counter *any* thought that comes to war with your mind. Romans 12:2 says, *"Do not conform any longer to the pattern of this world, but be transformed by the renewing of your mind. Then you will be able to test and approve what God's will is—his good, pleasing and perfect will."*

I value using strong mental images of The Word of God to battle against opponents that wage war against us in our mind. Jesus used stories that painted a picture in the minds of His listeners. I recommend you type a story that describes the horror Jesus Christ underwent at Calvary according to His Word and then meditate on it until the picture is seeded in your mind ready to be called to remembrance at any time. Within the first few seconds of the temptation, take your thoughts captive and demand of your mind to look steadfastly at the *crucified form of Jesus Christ.*

Let's say you just had a sexual thought that was inappropriate. Remember, you are in a war and your mind is the battlefield. Time is of great importance and you must respond quickly before you are overtaken by the enemy!

Speak to the ungodly thoughts and command them to depart from your mind. Jesus has given you the authority and power to do this. Next, call out to God, "God I need you. Help me!" Then demand of your mind according to Hebrews 12:2, to fix its gaze on **Christ on the cross.** *"Let us fix our eyes on Jesus, the author and perfecter of our faith, who for the joy set before him endured the cross, scorning its shame, and sat down at the right hand of the throne of God."*

Remember that although Christ was God, He was also fully man. Therefore, He experienced and endured the excruciating pain that would accompany such a horrifying death. According to Matthew Henry's Commentary, crucifixion was "so miserable a death that merciful princes appointed those who were condemned to it by the law, to be strangled first, and then nailed to the cross."[26] After studying what happened to Christ at Calvary, you should be able to visualize what He must have experienced that day.

For example, your description may be something like this–

Soldiers are mocking and spitting upon Him. He is gasping for breath causing His body to move up and down against the splintered cross beam. Splinters are seen in the deep cuts on His body and his skin is torn and hanging in strips caused from the beating He received. As he tries to pull away from the wood, His wrists are ripped by the massive spikes that were nailed through them. He screams with agony and pushes up with His feet to give some relief to His wrists. His pain is intensified even more as the bones and nerves in His pierced feet crush against each other. He screams again in anguish. His throat is dry and raw. Every time He throws his head back, the long thorns from the crown placed on his head, penetrate into his skull. His body is covered in blood. There He is at Calvary dying a bloody, cursed death of rejection, abandonment, shame and intolerable pain to pay the price to save you from your sin.

I believe this same picture can be used for winning battles with gossip, envy, lust, lying, drunkenness or any other temptation. Every time you start to "go there again"— to your weak area of temptation, whatever it might be – go back to that powerful picture of Calvary. See Him there and make the choice that this sin will not be one that contributes to His suffering there.

Remember that there is no time in the spiritual realm because time was created by God for man to live in. The eternal attribute of God indicates that God lives in one eternal present. Time has no affect on Him; He affects time. So when you consider that 2000 years ago and today are the same to God, you can see how bringing to your conscious mind a picture of the suffering of Jesus on the cross can be an effective deterrent to these attacks on our minds. Understand that I am not saying that Jesus is dying over again every time we sin. As discussed in a previous chapter, Christ paid an enormous price for my sin and the sins of all mankind – past, present and future. No other sacrifice is needed or ever will be needed. God knew all the sins that would ever be committed and put it all on Christ that day at Calvary. Just before taking His last breath, Christ said, "It is finished." Therefore, when you sin and repent, you are appropriating the forgiveness and cleansing that Jesus paid for 2000 years ago at Calvary. Seeing yourself right there before Him at Calvary when you are about to commit sin, however, is a powerful deterrent. We are thankful that He paid the price for those sins we do commit. But because we love Him, we cannot bear as we gaze upon Him on the cross, to allow the sin we struggle with today to be a part of the body of sin that caused His suffering then.

As you use this spiritual weapon in your battle against the temptations that wage war in your mind, you will find that you are no longer thinking about the sexual temptation and you are more careful about judging Susie or gossiping about her. You are no longer complaining about Jane and how she should have and could have handled things differently. (We always think our way is the only right way, don't we?) When you stand in your mind at Calvary and picture it as it really was for Jesus because of *your sin*, because of the sin *you are about to commit*, you will be empowered to resist that sin and gain victory over it. The answer to overcoming temptation is found at *Calvary*.

When the day comes when we are face to face with Jesus, no other pleasure, and nothing of this life will compare with the exhilaration of that moment! Nothing that goes on here on earth will matter to us at all! Nothing will ever mean so much as seeing God face to face. Nothing! That moment will be pure pleasure!

ROAD STOP:

Have you memorized passages of Scripture that you can call upon in times of battle? How long has it been since you meditated on Calvary? *It is time to return to Calvary and gain an understanding of the implications of the cross.*

I want to encourage you to visit Calvary more often. I believe your walk with Jesus will deepen if you do this.

Call on God and ask Him, *"Create in me a clean heart, O God, and renew a right, persevering, and steadfast spirit within me "(*Psalm 51:10 AMP).

God is merciful. Read the following verses and thank God for His mercy and forgiveness when you fall short.

"Although most of the many people who came from Ephraim, Manasseh, Issachar and Zebulun had not purified themselves, yet they ate the Passover, contrary to what was written. But Hezekiah prayed for them, saying, "May the LORD, who is good, pardon everyone who sets his heart on seeking God—the LORD, the God of his fathers—even if he is not clean according to the rules of the sanctuary. And the LORD heard Hezekiah and healed the people" (2 Chronicles 30:18-20).

Confess your sin, *calling it what it is* and receive forgiveness and cleansing according to 1 John 1:9.

CHAPTER EIGHTEEN

Sons of God

*"God blesses those who work for peace,
for they will be called the children of God"
(Matt 5:9 NLV)*

∽∾

What a great promise the above verse gives us to be "children of God!" Of course, those who are born again became His sons and daughters at the time of their spiritual birth, but this Scripture assures us that we will have our heavenly Father's **character** when we are *peacemakers*. It is talking about our coming to *resemble* our Father. 1 Corinthians 7:15 says, "God has called us to live in peace." He desires us to show others how to cooperate and get along with one another instead of how to compete and fight and see who can win the "I'm right - you are wrong" argument! So why is there so much friction in the church? Why are there wars and rumors of wars in the world? Why are people being killed and why are marriages being dissolved? Why are so many women and children suffering abuse, both physical and emotional? Almost every one seems to be fighting for *their rights*. People are *betraying* other people to get *where they want* and *what they want*, even in the church! Yes, even in the church. So what is the problem? One thing that is so important for us to accept as *women who walk with God* is that we are living in the world and yet we are not a part of it. The world persecuted Jesus and it will persecute us. Persecution hurts, but there is a precious reward that Jesus gives to those who are willing to undergo persecution with Him. That reward is that He blesses us by allowing us not only to share in His resurrection after we die, but we also share in His sufferings while we live. "I want to know Christ and the power of his resurrection and the fellowship of sharing in his sufferings, becoming like him in his death" (Phil 3:10).

Any one who walks with God will be persecuted at times. Jesus said, "if they persecuted Me, they will also persecute you (John 15:20b). We should not be surprised. The enemy of our souls will work in any way he can in any given situation even using people in the church in order to persecute God's children. He will do his best to get their focus off of Jesus. Satan would like to keep us distracted with persecution so that we do not fulfill God's purposes for our lives. But God is infinitely greater than Satan! Satan cannot stop what God is calling you to. It is so wonderful how our heavenly Father works through us to keep our attention on Him. The more we are persecuted, the stronger we become in Christ! The more Satan attacks us, the more grace God gives us to draw close to Him and the more of His heavenly character we absorb. The enemy just doesn't understand God's ways! My heart so cries out for unity within the body of Christ! I believe principles of conflict resolution and teaching concerning what a peacemaker looks like is desperately needed in our churches. After all, God says in Hosea 4:6 that His people are destroyed for lack of knowledge. People in general, and especially women, need to learn *how to have disagreements with one another without it breaking their relationships.*

The truth is that, we are going to have disagreements; we are going to have misunderstandings. This is inevitable. Because we are all human beings in process, we will have misunderstandings until the day Christ comes for us or we go to Him, whichever comes first. That disputes will arise is not the issue. The issue is how will we *handle* those misunderstandings? It is all right to disagree at times. We can still walk together in love. We can disagree on issues and agree that it is okay to disagree. Many times people are offended if someone doesn't think the same way concerning an issue as they do. There is no profit to becoming offended when everyone doesn't agree with you! Disagreements do NOT give a reason to divide, withdraw or run away. However, most disagreements are *simple differences of opinions* and we should accept that each of us is going to have one. Disagreements can even be healthy. When handled in love, conflict can release creativity and new prayer-fulness that births new ideas into a congregation or a relationship. Often it is a disagreement that brings to the surface deeper issues – items that threaten the stability of the relationship if not dealt with. There are times when issues need to be confronted in order to resolve a situation that is causing a break in the relationship. Sometimes this leads to a conflict. This is where the going gets tough. I have found this situation to be especially difficult for women when it arises in the church. We find it difficult to balance the Biblical commands to *forgive* and *forbear* with the need to speak up and confront. We ask, "How do we follow Christ and deal with conflict?" We wrongly think that we can't. Life has taught many women to aim for *peace whatever the cost*, but this attitude has caused no end of division in the body of Christ, whether seen in the natural realm or not. Women tend to be peacekeepers at the expense of peacemaking. They think they are taking the low road by saying nothing, however, this approach leaves an unmended break between the two that has not been resolved. The "stuffing it" technique is not the way of our Father when there is truly a division issue at hand. We should not be ***peacekeepers*** at the expense of ***peacemaking.*** Think about it. Do you see God as One who "stuffs" His feelings concerning matters? – Of course not!

So why do women find it so difficult to be honest with one another and talk things out openly? When we were young, most of us had no problem speaking out about our feelings. However, as we approached junior high school, we discovered that speaking truth about our feelings caused us to lose a relationship or two. We learned to "stuff our feelings" or to "run away" in order to avoid conflict and suffer rejection. The bottom line is that women tend to avoid conflict out of *fear of rejection* and *ridicule.* As Christian women, we deceive ourselves, get "religious", and call it "taking the low road". This is a serious problem we have in our lives and in our churches. The result is that relational disagreements and conflicts are constantly simmering below the surface, threatening to erupt at any moment.

When we become *God-centered* and we are bent on pursuing peace, then we are not so ruffled when someone disagrees with us. We are okay with it because we have learned to be *free in whom we are* and we are *able to allow others to be themselves* without demanding that they agree with us. We are free to pursue a unity that is real and true rather than superficial and artificial because, from our hearts, we desire agreement with fellow Christians that is based on God's Truth and instruction and not on anyone's personal opinion. It is difficult sometimes for a peacemaker when she is trying to walk in this kind of honesty with someone who has lived her life on the "stuff it and keep quiet so you won't be rejected" method. There are times that the other person is unable to hear your thoughts without becoming even more offended and the relationship becomes irreparably broken. For example, one counselee shared the following with me: "Many years ago I had noticed a change in the behavior of a working associate. There were a couple of distinct things that took place that really bothered me. I decided that I needed to lovingly and gently confront her and ask her if I had done something to offend her. My desire was to have the opportunity to apologize and make things right if I had hurt or offended her. I didn't want this break in our relationship that came out of nowhere to remain, and I hoped to discover what caused the break and to set things right. Believe me, I was scared to confront her. I was concerned that I might be rejected should I allow myself to be vulnerable in this way. But I decided *our relationship was worth the risk* of rejection. I desired to be a peacemaker. After all, the relationship was obviously suffering anyway and this was our only hope."

This particular experience did not produce the result she was hoping for. Her friend was unable to handle an honest exchange and responded defensively. She was unable to deal biblically with offenses that were separating them. Their relationship has never been the same – the intimacy once shared has been lost. The broken relationship grieves my counselee, but as the Apostle John said, "They went out from us, but they were not really of us; for if they had been of us, they would have remained with us; but they went out, in order that it might be shown that they all are not of us" (I John 2:19). In this Bible verse John is talking about *deceivers in the church*, but the **principle** held true in the relationship with my counselee and her co-worker friend. She had thought she was an intimate friend, but when she confronted some issues that were affecting their relationship, she realized her co-worker was not really her friend at all. God used the whole conflict to protect her from continuing to share intimately with the co-worker. Though the friendship was broken, my counselee was no longer deceived by her apparent friendliness. Remember, the relationship was *not* broken by the confrontation; it was broken by the perceived offense. Although the counselee desired reconciliation, her co-worker was content to hold her offense rather than talk it out.

Sisters, I want to give you a word of caution here. Avoid the temptation to use personal struggles a friend has shared with you during a time of confronting issues. Sometimes women will do this trying to prove that the other must be the one at fault.

After all, they have shared with you that they have issues. This is not peacemaking but waging war.

As you seek to be a peacemaker, remember that if an issue arises that you cannot let go of even after much prayer and soul-searching, if you stuff it you are not being a peacemaker. There may be a resemblance of peace on the exterior but the relationship will continue to deteriorate. This is a *"peace whatever the cost"* woman. Your relationship is broken and to be truly reconciled conversation must take place. In the example I just gave there was something that had come between the two women and one was not willing to talk about it. Since it was already evident in her behavior before she was approached about it that the relationship was already broken, it was appropriate to try and save the relationship by confronting the issue. Actually, this was the ONLY chance for a reconciliation for this situation. In this instance, it did not work. But I can promise you that *many more times* it does work. We should take the chance and pursue true peace and true reconciliation because God has called us to be **ministers of recon-**

ciliation, not *keepers of the peace*. God calls us to make peace a priority in our lives.

We read in Ephesians 4:3 *"make every effort to keep the unity of the Spirit through the bond of peace."* We can be the one to take the initiative and seek after peace. How do we do this? We can stand in the gap by praying. Ezekiel 22:30 says, *"I looked for a man among them who would build up the wall and stand before me in the gap on behalf of the land so I would not have to destroy it, but I found none."* Once we have prayed, we can reach out by making a phone call; making contact and setting up a meeting. Try to be as gentle and non-threatening as you can while explaining that your desire is to preserve your friendship. Don't call until you have fully forgiven any offenses you have against them so that your motives are pure and there are no accusations in your heart against them. If the other person refuses to seek reconciliation then you have done what you can and although this relationship may be lost, *your relation-ship with God is intact*. Continue to pray for them, and forgive them. Although because of your love for that person it can be difficult to do, at that point you must move on and press forward leaving the past behind. Watch over your heart and guard that a *spirit of rejection* does not enter in to you because of the unwillingness of the other party to reconcile with you; and know that you have done all that you can do. Remember that "Christ also accepted us to the glory of God" (Romans 15:7) and His acceptance is the one that really counts! Trust God with the situation and the person. Place both in the hands of God.

As you can see, it is important not to confuse a peace*maker* with a peace*keeper*. There is a huge difference and God calls us to be *peacemakers* not *peacekeepers*. A peace*keeper* is a woman who appeases through niceness and conflict avoidance. She pursues "peace whatever the cost", including the cost of trading an *intimate* relationship for a *superficial* one. Many times she pursues peace even at the risk of compromising hurting herself and what she believes. This is not the way that resembles our Father. It is very difficult for me to form intimate relationships with women who are peacekeepers. *You never know* *what is true in the relationship.* Peacekeepers can be offended with you about something and you will never know unless you find out through the grape-vine. You notice something is not right but you do not know what it is and you are not given the oppor-tunity to make it right. In contrast, I appreciate my friends confronting me when they are bothered by something that concerns me because I would never intentionally hurt any one. This honesty and open-ness is an act of love towards me. They are showing me they are willing to invest their time and energy into our friendship. When an issue threatens to sepa-rate us, they give me an opportunity to talk through my perspective on the issue and to explain myself in the misunderstanding. Sometimes it becomes the opportunity to recognize that I am wrong and they have given me the opportunity to recognize that and apologize to them. "*As **iron sharpens iron**, So a man **sharpens** the countenance of his friend* (Proverbs 27:17). Sometimes they are able to see the heart in the situation and realize there has been a misunder-standing perhaps due to faulty perceptions that dwell within each of us. These faulty perceptions are what cause so many misunderstandings in our communications with one another. When we commit to principles such as these, we prevent the enemy from being able to cause division of which he is a master. I give the same respect and love towards all my friends as well. This is the only way for a true, intimate friendship to develop. This same principle is true for having a great marriage. Have you realized yet that nobody is perfect? All of us must have grace for and walk in love with one another. Relationships grow stronger and healthier when there is a freedom to share your true feelings, even when they don't make complete sense and even when they are unjustified. This freedom to share is necessary in order to have a genuine reconciliation between two individuals.

To be the peacemakers that God has called us to be, friends should feel free to come to us and share concerning hurt feelings. We should then receive them in love, apologize, explain any misunderstanding, and assure them of our intent. I would want to tell her how much I love her and assure her that I will do my best not to let this *same thing* happen again. I will appreciate that she has revealed this tender area of her soul with me, trusting me as a friend and woman of God, and making herself vulnerable to me not to reject her for it. When we approach relationships in this way we have actually come to know one another even better and our relationship grows stronger. Of course, it takes two believers who are mature enough in the Lord to see past their own emotional issues, of which most of us have due to our fallen natures, to reach a true reconciliation. Many women inside and out of the church struggle with thoughts and feelings of rejection, guilt, worthlessness and a need to perform and a need to be more. Many times those suffering with a fear of rejection are overly sensitive and have the tendency to read rejection and criticism into even the most innocent interactions and hurt feelings flow to the surface. The other party usually doesn't have a clue to what has happened.

Because I love my friend and because I now know more about her and her sensitivities, I will attempt to be careful not to hurt her in this same way again. For the sake of Christ, it is important to be careful not to mistake the resemblance of peace as real peace. Conflict may be hidden and deterred because the divisive issues have not been confronted. But they are still there. This false peace leaves a crack in the relationship. It is hidden, but eventually that crack can turn into a permanent break beyond repair. This happens over and over again even within the body of Christ. Churches split, friends are lost and the body of Christ suffers as does the advancement of God's kingdom. Are you guilty of running from an uncomfortable conversation that needs to take place in order that your relationship may be reconciled? If so, you are not being a peacemaker, but you may be contributing to *deepening* the crack in the relationship. This is not God's way and it results in anxiety. Where there is no peace there is no satisfaction.

A peacemaker is one who understands the importance of ***unity*** and desires to ***shine light*** into the situation and ***redeem*** the relationship just as Christ has redeemed us. She is one who will make a **plea for peace**, asking for the warring factions to lay down their arms, soften their hearts, and *believe that God is able to reconcile the relationship* if we just are willing to allow Him the opportunity. 2 Corinthians 5:20 says, *"we implore you on Christ's behalf: Be reconciled to God!"* When we are at war with one another, **our relationship with God is broken** as well. I ask you, is it worth it? I think not. When we disagree with someone's thoughts, feelings or values, we may need to enter into a discussion concerning the issue. Matthew 18:15-17 gives us clear instruction on handling conflicts of this nature. *"If your brother sins against you go and show him his fault, just between the two of you. If he listens to you, you have won your brother over. But if he will not listen, take one or two others along, so that 'every matter may be established by the testimony of two or three witnesses. If he refuses to listen to them, tell it to the church; and if he refuses to listen even to the church, treat him as you would a pagan or a tax collector."*

To truly come to a place of reconciliation when an offense has occurred whether through a misunderstanding or an actual difference in values, or due to a sinful attitude, this step of confronting in love cannot be avoided.

Of course, there are those times when we should just *forgive* and *forbear*. For example, we all have little idiosyncrasies that bother us or that bother us when we see them in others. God has made each of us uniquely unique for His purposes. Sometimes there are things we just have to accept about another and we continue on by the grace of God. However, when a wounding seems to have taken place in your soul then you need to talk to the person who wounded you with an attitude to reconcile. You simply confront them in love concerning the issue saying something like, "I am bothered by something I heard the other day and would like to ask you about it." Or, "I am bothered by something you said the other day (or did the other day) and would like to ask you to share with me why you would say that (or do that); or what you meant by that." When we are offended, most of the time the person who offended us has no idea that they have done so. It simply is "*SIMPLY A MISUNDERSTANDING*". What was perceived to have been intended to hurt us is not what the person thought or intended at all. For your own sake and for the sake of others, take the time to learn to honestly communicate in love your hurt feelings and stop jumping to conclusions about situations. We have got to quit allowing the enemy of God and of the family of God, to get away with his tactics; using our fallen natures against us to listen to him as he twists things as prince of the power of the air. We can have victory in Christ! We need to rise up and commit to one another that we will not allow this to happen! The pain you are experiencing could be instantly gone by having the light of the truth shed on the situation. Darkness is dispelled. And please don't be eager to run to others concerning the offense. Only the person(s) involved are able to shed *true* light and truth into the situation that concerns you.

Another important part of this process is that once we hear the other person's explanation, we need to be willing to *receive* it as truth and put away the lie we have believed that is causing us pain as well as causing a break in our relationship with one another and with God. Why do you want to hang on to the hurtful thought instead of believing in your sister's love for you? We need to learn to forgive others for not being and acting in perfect harmony with us and our ways of being and doing. How prideful we can be, thinking we are RIGHT to think and feel the way we do and expecting others to think and feel the same way. We all have our unique personalities from birth and unique experiences of which we filter through. We all have fallen natures. I am convinced that a *commitment to truthfulness, forgiveness and the giving of grace to one another is at the very heart of walking in love and being a peacemaker.*

Ken Sande, in his book "The Peace Maker" gives us a checklist to follow. "Whenever you are involved in a conflict, you may apply the four basic principles of peacemaking by asking yourself these questions:

*"**Glorify God**: How can I please and honor the Lord in this situation?*

***Get the log out of your eye:** How can I show Jesus' work in me by taking responsibility* for my contribution to this conflict?

Gently restore: How can I lovingly serve others by helping them take responsibility for their contribution to this conflict?

Go and be reconciled: How can I demonstrate the forgiveness of God and encourage a reasonable solution to this conflict?" [26]

I will say it again, not to speak up to the "offender" causes the relationship to become fractured between the two parties but not only between the two friends, but also between the *offended* and *God*. Nothing is worth that. God loves peace and sends us into the world to mend broken relationships. As we learn to walk as peacemakers, we truly begin to resemble our Father as "daughters" of God. Oh, my sister, don't you want to hear Him say, "That's my girl. You're growing up and you sure resemble your Daddy."

ROAD STOP:

Are you guilty of running from an uncomfortable conversation that needs to take place in order that your relationship may be reconciled? If so, you are not being a peacemaker. You are allowing the crack in that relationship to grow deeper.

Are you guilty of running to others to talk about the situation, leadership or not leadership, under the pretense of getting counsel? If so, you are not doing anything that can bring reconciliation in your relationship. I know this sounds hard, but the truth of the matter is that you are *simply gossiping* and grieving the Holy Spirit. Repent and make an appointment to talk with the person you are offended with. Do all that is in your power to pursue reconciliation and *be called a child of God*!

CHAPTER NINETEEN

Happiness and Persecution

*"Blessed and happy and enviably fortunate and
spiritually prosperous (in the state in which the
born-again child of God enjoys and finds satisfaction in God's favor and salvation, regardless of his
outward conditions) are those who are persecuted
for righteousness' sake (for being and doing right),
for theirs is the kingdom of heaven!"*
(Matthew 5:10 AMP)

∽✐∾

When *your commitment to God provokes
persecution*, you are blessed, and the
persecution can drive you even deeper into God's
kingdom! That's what Jesus meant when He spoke
the words that introduce this chapter. Then He added,
just to make sure everyone understood exactly
what He meant, *"blessed (happy, to be envied, and*

spiritually prosperous—with life-joy and satisfaction in God's favor and salvation, regardless of your outward conditions) are you when people revile you and persecute you and say all kinds of evil things against you falsely on My account" (Matthew 5:11, AMP). In other words, every time people put you down or throw you out or speak lies about you, it is to discredit Christ. The truth is too close for comfort and they are uncomfortable with you. *"be glad and supremely joyful, for your reward in heaven is great (strong and intense), for in this same way people persecuted the prophets who were before you"* *(Matthew 5:12 AMP).*

"but they mocked God's messengers, despised his words and scoffed at his prophets until the wrath of the LORD was aroused against his people and there was no remedy" (2 Chronicles 36:16).

We don't find it easy to think about, but *suffering* does have a place in the life of a believer. Neither Jesus nor the Apostle Paul promised their followers a life of ease or public approval. In fact, what we see through their teachings is that there are two groups of people in the world: Those *who belong to Jesus* and *those who do not*. Those who do not belong to Him hate those who do. John 15:18-21 tells us, *"If the world hates you, keep in mind that it hated me first. If you belonged to the world, it would love you as its own. As it is, you do not belong to the world, but I have chosen you out of the world. That is why the world hates you. Remember the words I spoke to you: 'No servant is greater than his master.' If they persecuted me, they will persecute you also. If they obeyed my teaching, they will obey yours also. They will treat you this way because of my name, for they do not know the One who sent me."* Philippians 1:29 says, *"for it has been granted to you on behalf of Christ not only to believe on him, but also to suffer for him."* In other words, suffering is a *gift* that comes to us along with salvation. Paul writes in Philippians 3:10, *"I want to know Christ and the power of his resurrection and the fellowship of sharing in his sufferings, becoming like him in his death."* Jesus has given us His example of how to respond to suffering and adversity that come from the circumstances of life in a way that transforms the adversity or suffering into glory to God. Romans 8:16-18 tells us that we are co-heirs with Christ if indeed we share in His sufferings in order that we may also share in His glory. We read in 1 Peter 4:12-16,

> *"dear friends, do not be surprised at the painful trial you are suffering, as though something strange were happening to you. But rejoice that you participate in the sufferings of Christ, so that you may be overjoyed when his glory is revealed. If you are insulted because of the name of Christ, you are blessed, for the Spirit of glory and of God rests on you. If you suffer, it should not be as a murderer or thief or any other kind of criminal, or even as a meddler. However, if you suffer as a Christian, do not be ashamed, but praise God that you bear that name."*

It should not be strange to us to suffer persecution, insults and to have lies spoken against us. Suffering as a Christian goes along with bearing His name. We can be content in the midst of our suffering because we know that as we *share in His sufferings*, we also will *share in His glory*. It is in suffering that the *reality of our faith* is made known to us. It is also in suffering that the *power of the resurrected Christ is manifested* in the life of the Christian for others to see and be drawn to Him.

We can also be content in our sufferings knowing that such *sufferings purify us*, resulting in our becoming more like Christ. 2 Corinthians 4:11-18,

"for we who are alive are always being given over to death for Jesus' sake, so that his life may be revealed in our mortal body. So then, death is at work in us, but life is at work in you. It is written: 'I believed; therefore I have spoken.' With that same spirit of faith we also believe and therefore speak, because we know that the one who raised the Lord Jesus from the dead will also raise us with Jesus and present us with you in his presence. All this is for your benefit, so that the grace that is reaching more and more people may

cause thanksgiving to overflow to the glory of God. Therefore we do not lose heart. Though outwardly we are wasting away, yet inwardly we are being renewed day by day. For our light and momentary troubles are achieving for us an eternal glory that far out weighs them all. So we fix our eyes not on what is seen, but on what is unseen. For what is seen is temporary, but what is unseen is eternal."

There are three very important things to remember when you find yourself in a season of suffering or persecution. First, God promises that the suffering will never be more than you can bear. 1 Cor 10:13, *"no temptation has seized you except what is common to man. And God is faithful; he will not let you be tempted beyond what you can bear. But when you are tempted, he will also provide a way out so that you can stand up under it."* Secondly, The Lord Jesus Christ is with you and will never leave you or forsake you. Hebrews 13:5 says, *"Keep your lives free from the love of money and be content with what*

*you have, because God has said, never will I leave
you; never will I forsake you."*

And thirdly, the truth is that *your life cannot be
taken* because it is held in God's hands. Hebrews 2:14
says, *"since the children have flesh and blood, he
too shared in their humanity so that by his death he
might destroy him who holds the power of death that
is, the devil"*; Rev 1:18 says, *"I am the Living One;
I was dead, and behold I am alive for ever and ever!
And I hold the keys of death and Hades."* So how
does a woman who walks with God with life-joy and
satisfaction in God's favor and salvation, regardless
of the outward conditions respond to persecution and
suffering? She is content in the midst of challenging
circumstances of any kind, because her focus is on
God and her relationship with Him. Without keeping
your eyes on Jesus, you will not be able to respond in
a manner that will transform suffering into the glory
of God. It is out of your *intimate relationship* with
Him that you will be able to respond this way. It is
because of your relationship with Him that you are
able to respond.

We are able to respond: (1) **Towards God** *with rejoicing*, counting it joy and giving thanks. 1 Peter 4:12 tells us, "dear friends, do not be surprised at the painful trial you are suffering, as though something strange were happening to you." (2) **Towards the person(s) causing the suffering**, *without terror or fear* or intimidation (1 Peter 3:14-15). Then we can see in 1 Peter 2:20-25 Christ's example of *how we are to respond to suffering* – *"but how is it to your credit if you receive a beating for doing wrong and endure it? But if you suffer for doing good and you endure it, this is commendable before God. To this you were called, because Christ suffered for you, leaving you an example that you should follow in his steps. He committed no sin, and no deceit was found in his mouth. When they hurled their insults at him, he did not retaliate; when he suffered, he made no threats. Instead, he entrusted himself to him who judges justly. He himself bore our sins in his body on the tree, so that we might die to sins and live for righteousness; by his wounds we have been healed. For you were like sheep going astray, but now you* *have returned to the Shepherd and Overseer of your souls."*

When we are living a life without satisfaction, our families suffer as proper nurturing is lacking. The lost do not want anything to do with Christ if you are a picture of what will happen to them if they come to Him. God is not glorified in our lives when we behave like this. But because of Christ, you can be satisfied even in the midst of challenging circumstances. You can count it joy to share in the sufferings of Christ *because you know you will also share in His glory.* As you respond out of your love toward God by enduring, by not retaliating, by **not** making threats, and by entrusting yourself to the One who judges fairly, you can know that the results will be eternal. God will be glorified. You will be purified. Others will be justified. This is the way of a woman who is walking with God with His favor on her life.

ROAD STOP:

When in the middle of persecution can you see how God is glorified as you turn to Him, trust in Him and allow Him to be your strength and refuge? Ask God to be your tower of refuge and strength and He will be there for you. He will hide you in the shadow of His wings until the danger passes.

CHAPTER TWENTY

Knowing and Accepting
Who God Is

*"Know, recognize, and understand therefore this
day and turn your mind and heart to it that the Lord
is God in the heavens above and upon the earth
beneath; there is no other"*
Deuteronomy 4:39 (NIV)

In order to experience genuine satisfaction, it is imperative you come to know God. Of course God is so awesome that you can never know Him fully, but you can continuously pursue and progressively know more of Him. As you do this, God will reveal Himself to you so that you know, that you know, you can trust Him. Pursuing God is the only way to develop confidence in God. Without confidence in God's *character,* confidence in *His love* and confidence in *His ways*, it is impossible to truly experience fulfillment and satisfaction in life. Unless you **trust God**, you will not be able to **accept the things** in life that you **do not understand.** It is only as you **know God** that you can have **peace and confidence** no matter *who you are*, no matter *where you find yourself*, and no matter *what circumstance is surrounding you.*

How do you get to know God enough that you may trust Him? Daily time spent in prayer is essential to knowing God. As you pray, don't forget to *be still* and allow *Him to talk to you.* So many times we are so busy talking that He cannot get a word in edgewise! As you spend time with Him, your knowledge of Him as well as your relationship with Him will deepen.

It is also important to spend time in the Bible because God has revealed all that we need to know about Him and His ways in His written Word to us. Nature leaves man without excuse concerning the truth that there is a God, but only in the Bible can you come to know the character of God. We can know *how He will respond* in various types of situations, because He is the same yesterday, today and forever. You will discover that *He is unchanging* and *He is always faithful.* What peace this revelation brings to our souls!

As you grow in your obedience to Him, you will discover that your knowledge about Him will increase. You see, *God rewards our obedience with deeper illumination of Himself!* Studying the names of God is another great way to grow in your relationship and knowledge of God. God reveals His character through the names He gives to Himself. Just as we can know more about a woman when she is called "mother" or "wife", we can know more about God as we study His names and their meaning. There are several good books in the Christian Bookstores about the names of God. One that has meant a lot to me is: <u>My Father's Names</u> by Elmer L. Towns.

"He is Jehovah Roi, the One who cares for all the needs of His sheep. He is El Shaddai, the God who supplies all my needs. He is El Elyon, the Possessor of Heaven and earth. He is great to the superlative degree. He is El Olam, the Everlasting God available to His people throughout the ages, yet remains a mystery and a secret to mere human minds. He is El Gibbor. In battle He is a divine Warrior and in uncertain times He is a divine Rock. God always supports His children with His strength *unless* they insist on trusting on their own strength. He is Jehovah Melek a benevolent King who establishes laws for the good of His subjects and He deserves our total obedience. As Jehovah Sabaoth, He is the Commander of the angels. He sends these angels to guard and protect us from harm and as we follow Him into battle, we know the outcome is certain to be Victorious! As our divine Master, Adonai, we can expect Him to supply us with all the resources and provision we need in order to live out every situation He allows us to be in; and to carry out all that He calls us to do. God is Elohim, the God who is the source of all there is. He is life, person, spirit, self-existent, One, unchangeable and unlimited. And as the plural Elohim implies, God is three-in-one, the Trinity. God is the self-existent God who is the eternal source of life—He who will be who He will be, whose existence depends on no other. God also desires to be known to His children by the intimate name of Pater as our loving Father. Through Christ we are invited not to cower before Him in fear but to enter into an intimate family relationship with Him."[28]

When a Christian is confident of who God is and when she accepts God for who He is, satisfaction will result. Until then, you will always be second-guessing God, expecting Him to respond differently to situations in your life, and you will never be satisfied.

Growing in an understanding of His love, sovereignty, omnipotence (all-powerful), omniscience (all knowing), omnipresence (everywhere present) and His immutability (unchanging nature) has proven for me to be crucial in building my confidence and accepting His hand on my life. Understanding and believing by faith that **God is Who He says He is** will bring you to a point of acceptance concerning His governing your life; concerning accepting the circumstances you will find yourself in at various seasons of life; concerning accepting those things that you do not understand; concerning accepting the things you cannot change; and concerning accepting how valuable you are to God. How significant every detail of your life is to Him!

God is *Love. "And so we know and rely on the love God has for us. God is Love. Whoever lives in love lives in God, and God in him"* (1 John 4:16). Because God is Love, He is forever giving of Himself to others to bring blessings to them. Love is not a garment He wears that can be taken off. The Bible tells us that He Himself is Love. He cannot divest Himself of it. Therefore, everything God does and everything God allows comes forth from love because He is Love. Have you ever known anyone who would die for their enemy? God the Son left heaven and came to earth as a man. He was brutally beaten, rejected, scorned and crucified because He desired to reconcile you to Himself. He did this when you were at enmity with Him. Now that is love beyond our comprehension! It is necessary to accept His love by faith. This is a love that never fails! This is a love that never fades! This is a love you can count on! Who has or ever will demonstrate their love toward you as He has done? Romans 5:8, *"But God demonstrates his own love for us in this: While we were still sinners, Christ died for us."*

God is supreme in power, rank, authority and work. There is no one and nothing like God. He is supreme over all the earth and everything in it. There is no greater power or authority. Everything that exists was created by Him for His purposes. He is all-powerful and in control of every situation. Isaiah 45:5-7,

> *"I am the LORD, and there is no other;*
> *apart from me there is no God.*
> *I will strengthen you,*
> *though you have not acknowledged me,*
> *so that from the rising of the sun*
> *to the place of its setting*
> *men may know there is none besides me.*
> *I am the LORD, and there is no other.*
> *I form the light and create darkness,*
> *I bring prosperity and create disaster;*
> *I, the LORD, do all these things."*

When I say that God is *sovereign*, I am saying that nothing happens in the heavens and earth without God's permission. Our God rules! The reality of this should bring to you a sense of security like you have never experienced before! Daniel 4:25b-26 says, *"Seven times will pass by for you until you acknowledge that the Most High is sovereign over the kingdoms of men and gives them to anyone he wishes. The command to leave the stump of the tree with its roots means that your kingdom will be restored to you when you acknowledge that Heaven rules".*

And because He is Love, we can know that everything that God allows to happen will only be allowed to happen if He can use it for good according to His sovereign, eternal purpose and plan for our lives. Does this mean we will understand it? I can tell you that we will not understand everything that God does or allows in our lives. Many times we want to ask, "How can any good come out of this circumstance? But when we know God, we know that His character requires of Him that He turn everything to good to accomplish His purposes. Knowing this, we can accept by faith His plan for our lives and we can be satisfied in it.

Although God is sovereign, man still has free will and is accountable to God for His choices. God's plans are so sovereign and He is so powerful that He can intervene in our choices and circumstances to perfect His plan. In other words, God rules and He also over-rules, and no man, angel, demon or circumstance of life can stop His plan from coming to pass. Although God has given me free will, there are times when in His sovereign love and grace He intervenes and overrules my choice. Praise the Lord! At other times, however, He allows me to make wrong choices. But when He allows this, He has a plan and purpose to use it for my good in bringing me closer to Him and molding me into His image. And my wrong choices will not thwart the plan of God in any way, shape or form! God's very essence is Love and He rules supremely over all even in the area of correction and discipline. Hebrews 12:10 tells us that the Father's discipline is a manifestation of His love for His children: *"Our fathers disciplined us for a little while as they thought best; but God disciplines us for our good, that we may share in his holiness."*

One of God's moral attributes is *goodness*. God is the only and final standard for goodness. Therefore, everything He does is worthy of approval. In Luke 18:19b, Jesus declares *"No one is good — except God alone."* We can rest in the love and goodness of God! What confidence this gives us in living out the circumstances of our lives. And *it is this **confidence in God** that enables us to live as **satisfied women.***

A few years ago I was at the beach with a group of women for a ladies' retreat. One morning my friend and I waited on the elevator with no one in sight. Then just as we stepped onto the elevator, there was suddenly a large group of senior citizens hurrying behind us to catch the elevator. As they stepped onto the elevator, I was forced to against the back wall. As they continued to pile in I cried out, "No". The elevator door closed. I knew in my spirit that the elevator could not safely hold so many people.

As the elevator began to descend, I became very hot and was finding it difficult to breath. I looked to the ceiling and there was no fan in the elevator. Needless to say, with all the bodies packed in the elevator during the hottest time of the year without air conditioning or a fan, it was like a hot sauna! The floor numbers were descending and we came to our floor where the elevator was to stop. Unfortunately my concern became a reality. The elevator passed by the floor and stopped between floors. We were over-loaded! And, we were stuck!

Right then and there I had to choose whether to panic or to trust God. It was one of those opportunities when the reality of your faith is proven or not proven. My friend was pressed against the elevator phone. She squeezed it out of its cradle and called the emergency number. There was no answer! She called again. No answer again!

The air was thinning very quickly. There were too many people for the little air that remained. I began to talk to God. I said, "I know you are sovereign and all-powerful. I know you can get us out of this elevator if You want to. Father, if it is not our time to come meet you face to face, then I am asking

You to save us. If it is Your will for us to come to You, then Your will be done." I could see an image of light as I was talking to God, and it was as though I was in another place. I asked Him if there were any sins I was unaware of that I should repent of. I was at perfect peace while chatting with the Lord, knowing that my God was in control of all things and that nothing could *accidentally* take my life without His permission.

People were beginning to panic. We had had no success reaching anyone by phone. My friend began to sing a song to the Lord and we all began to join in, even though we knew we were using more air by singing. We continued trying the phone and FINALLY someone answered IT. Within seconds someone was prying the doors open and assisting us out of the elevator!

During that experience, God COMFORTED ME concerning some difficult things that were going on in my life. I had just experienced betrayal by my best friend. That was a difficult trial for me. I did not understand how she could say, "don't take it personal.

It's just business." Needless to say, I was depressed in my spirit, feeling a little rejected and a lot hurt. I had experienced betrayal by my former husband as well so this was quite devastating. I wondered why those I loved continued to betray me. God bathed me in His love and told me I was His workmanship and He was well pleased with me. He told me I was valuable to Him. He told me He had plans for me and it was not yet time to come to be with Him.

Just as our conversation ended, someone answered the phone and within seconds men were at the elevator door beginning to pry it open! God touched me that day and infused a sense of significance into my very soul! I felt that He had stopped the elevator just to speak to "little 'ole me"! I wonder who else in that elevator He may have been speaking to at the very same time. It could be that the enemy of our souls had planned to hurt all of us on that elevator that day. God allowed him to go so far but no further. Perhaps it occurred, just to get me into a place where He could talk to me and I could listen. My God rules;

and my life is held in His hands and His hands alone! If you are a Christian, the same holds true for you!

I will tell you now about my heavenly Father's *omnipresence*. God is everywhere simultaneously! There is not a place where God is not. Psalm 139:5 says about God, "*You both precede and follow me. You place your hand of blessing on my head.*" Realizing that God is with you wherever you are is a great comfort. God's omnipresence insures His power. Because He is always with His children, He is able to work in their lives at all times, working in all of us at the same time. He is there when you are lonely, when you are afraid, when you are weak. He brings you His love, comfort and strength. He guides you when you don't know where to go. He is always with you. He will always be right there! Hebrews 13:5, "*Never will I leave you; never will I forsake you.*"

Another wonderful truth concerning God is that He is *immutable*—**unchanging!** He will never be more than what He is right now and has always been, and He will never be less. He is all in all. God spoke to Malachi as written in Malachi 3:6, "*I the LORD* *do not change."* Change happens to us without our consent. Our circumstances change and the people in our lives change. But we can be satisfied and at peace knowing that our God NEVER changes!

God is **all-powerful (omnipotent)**. He doesn't derive power from another source but He is the source of His Own power. *"For he spoke, and it came to be; he commanded, and it stood firm" (Psalm 33:9).* There is nothing more powerful than God.

> *"Your throne was established long ago;*
> *you are from all eternity.*
> *The seas have lifted up, O LORD,*
> *the seas have lifted up their voice;*
> *the seas have lifted up their pounding waves.*
> *Mightier than the thunder of the great waters,*
> *mightier than the breakers of the sea—*
> *the LORD on high is mighty"*
> *(Psalm 93:2-4)*

As a child of God, you are able to draw on the power of your Father. *"I can do everything through him who gives me strength"* (Philippians 4:13). It is the unlimited strength of our all-powerful God that works everything for good to those called. *"... we know that in all things God works for the good of* those who love him, who have been called according to his purpose"(Romans 8:28).

Our God is also **omniscient or all knowing**. Wayne Grudem in his book, Bible Doctrine, defines God's knowledge as follows: *"God fully knows Himself and all things actual and possible in one simple and eternal act."*[29] God's knowledge never changes or grows. He has always been and will always be omniscient. God has known all things from all eternity— that which would happen and that which He would do. God knows everything! He knows everything about you and He is totally aware of His creation. He knows your thoughts and desires. Psalm 139:1-18 confirms this message,

"O LORD, you have searched me
    and you know me.
You know when I sit and when I rise;
    you perceive my thoughts from afar.
You discern my going out and my lying down;
    you are familiar with all my ways.
Before a word is on my tongue

you know it completely, O LORD.

You hem me in—behind and before;

you have laid your hand upon me.

Such knowledge is too wonderful for me,

too lofty for me to attain.

Where can I go from your Spirit?

Where can I flee from your presence?

If I go up to the heavens, you are there;

if I make my bed in the depths, you are there.

If I rise on the wings of the dawn,

if I settle on the far side of the sea,

Even there your hand will guide me;

your right hand will hold me fast.

If I say, "Surely the darkness will hide me

and the light become night around me,"

Even the darkness will not be dark to you;

the night will shine like the day,

for darkness is as light to you.

For you created my inmost being;

you knit me together in my mother's womb.

I praise you because I am fearfully and wonder-

fully made;

your works are wonderful,

I know that full well.

My frame was not hidden from you

when I was made in the secret place.

When I was woven together in the depths of

the earth,

your eyes saw my unformed body.

All the days ordained for me

were written in your book

before one of them came to be.

How precious to me are your thoughts, O God!

How vast is the sum of them!

Were I to count them,

they would outnumber the grains of sand.

When I awake,

I am still with you."

As a Christian woman develops a deeper under-standing of God by studying His attributes and char-acter as revealed in Scripture, her confidence in God deepens. Understanding that God loves you, is always with you, is all-powerful, all-knowing, unchanging, and that He sovereignly rules over all heaven and earth, she finds every reason to be *satisfied*. She realizes that she is in good hands—the hands of God!

ROAD STOP:

Although some *satisfaction* can be a result of understanding Who God is, it is in the **accepting** of who God is and the seeking of a relationship with Him that brings **genuine satisfaction** and peace to a Christian.

Do you struggle with accepting the difficult times in your life?

Does it bring you peace to know that all things in heaven and earth are being governed by a loving God who rules and overrules according to the counsel of His sovereign will? What does it mean to you that God will fulfill His purpose and plan for your life?

Do you trust God with your life? Have you received His love for you?

CHAPTER TWENTY-ONE

Knowing Your Value

*"But you are the ones **chosen by God, chosen for the high calling** of priestly work, **chosen to be a holy people, God's instruments** to do his work and **speak out for him**, to tell others of the night-and-day difference he made for you—"*
(1 Peter 2:9 MSG).

⤳⤳

In the previous chapter we established that genuine satisfaction is not available without your *accepting Who God is!* And, of course, *to accept* God for Who He is, you have *to know* Who He is. Another area of acceptance that we need to address is the area of *accepting yourself.* Since the fall of man, men and women have struggled in the area of self acceptance. Striving for self worth and self esteem continues to be an issue within the church as well as outside of it.

In order to be a satisfied woman, however, you must learn to accept yourself.

As 1 Peter 2:9 states above, God chose you. He picked you out even before you were formed in your mother's womb, and He did so knowing every single detail of what your future would hold. "For you created my inmost being; you knit me together in my mother's womb" (Psalm 139:13). This holy, sovereign, all-powerful, all-knowing God Who is Creator of all that exists, picked you out to be His daughter. He knew your every thought and action, both good and evil, even before you experienced them yourself, and *He chose you anyway*!

The fact that God has chosen you is what makes you significant! God chose you and He now says that you are righteous. You ask, "How can this be?" The whole truth is that He has chosen you and you have been made righteous because He says so. You do not have to understand it; you just have to accept it. The Christian walk is a walk of faith and it is also by faith that you must accept that you are a righteous child of God!

You are not whom your father, mother or any other relative or friend has said you are. Even if they are continuing to say negative things about you, you are still the person God created you to be. You are not whom your boss or co-workers say you are. You are not whom your teachers told you that you were. You are whom God says you are and He says you are righteous! He says He has chosen you for a high calling! You are significant to God and He is the One Whose opinion really counts! He says He has chosen you to be holy and to be His instrument and voice on the earth!

Is there any person or any thing on this earth who is greater, who has more power, who has more fame, who has more significance than the One who holds the stars and planets in the universe and sets the boundaries of the oceans? Is there anyone or any thing that would carry a higher worth than He Who is the King of Kings and Lord of Lords? There is not! You must accept by faith whom God says you are if you are going to walk as a genuinely satisfied woman!

True satisfaction also comes as you realize that *God has made you for a purpose.*

You are wonderfully complex and wonderfully unique. There is no one else in the universe that is just like you. The way you look, the way you feel, the way you think — you may not understand yourself, but God does. It is not by accident that you were born where you were born or that you have the interests that you have. God was at work in planning every area of your life even before you were born. He has been at work forming you to be who you are. And He designed you wonderfully unique for the special purpose He has for you to fulfill on the earth. That's right: God has a plan and a purpose for your life on earth; and He has made you uniquely you in order that you can walk out His plan.

2 Cor 3:5 tells us that our competence comes from God. You have special abilities that your sister may not have. One of my good friends is the most wonderful cook. I am doing good not to burn the oatmeal! However, my friend is not good on the computer while I can keyboard pretty well. My

computer skills have come in handy while writing this book! God gave specific abilities to each of us for *His* purposes.

God also has allowed experiences in your life—some good and some bad. But He has used all these experiences in molding you into the woman He desires you to be. Romans 8:28, *"And we know that in all things God works for the good of those who love him, who have been called according to his purpose."* God is always with you and although He is not the cause of everything that happens to you, He does allow those things to happen and He will cause good to come out of them. Sometimes there are experiences allowed in our lives that will not only be used in shaping us, but God will also use that experience for equipping us to help others who are hurting. 2 Cor 1:4, *"He comes alongside us when we go through hard times, and before you know it, he brings us alongside someone else who is going through hard times so that we can be there for that person just as God was there for us"*(NKJV).

The greatest proof of your value is that God left His lofty place in heaven to come to earth as a man and to live as a man in order to die for you. If you have not yet accepted God's gift of salvation, please turn back to chapter two of this book to read about salvation. You can enter His Kingdom right now. All you need to do is to recognize you are a sinner in need of a Savior. Ask God to forgive you of your sin and tell Him you accept Jesus Christ as your Lord and Savior.

You have **worth** because God gave His life, which had **infinite value** for you. Who would pay such a high price for something of no value? You, my sister, are more valuable than anything on the earth!

The following Scripture agrees with 1 Peter 2:9:

"And they sang a new song:
Worthy! Take the scroll, open its seals.
Slain! Paying in blood, you bought men and
*   women,*
Bought them back from all over the earth,
Bought them back for God.
Then you made them a Kingdom,
*   Priests for our God,*
Priest-Kings to rule over the earth"
*   (Revelation 5:9-10 The Message Bible)*

God has declared that you are a royal priesthood! Because you are a child of God, you have personal access to the throne room of heaven. Hebrew 4:16 says, "Let us then approach the throne of grace with confidence, so that we may receive mercy and find grace to help us in our time of need."

The truth is that God didn't choose you because of anything you did or didn't do. He didn't choose you for any reason known to us. We only know that He chose to love us and He desired to keep His promise to Abraham whose descendants we are if we have faith in Jesus Christ. God spoke to Israel in Deuteronomy:

"GOD wasn't attracted to you and didn't choose you because you were big and important—the fact is, there was almost nothing to you. He did it out of sheer love, keeping the promise he made to your ancestors" (Deuteronomy 7:7-8 The Message Bible).

As we talk about developing healthy self-esteem and recognizing your self-worth, I want to point out that I am not talking about having confidence in yourself *without* God. What I am talking about is having confidence in the person *God* made you to be. In actuality, your confidence is in God, not in you. Paul said, "I can do all things through Christ who strengthens me" (Philippians 4:13).

Moses doubted his own strength and ability to carry out the work God had called him to. You can read the full story in the book of Exodus. Moses began his ministry without confidence in himself. But he did have confidence in God! It is because of God's grace and power that we are able to do the things He calls us to do! We must recognize and accept the limitations God has put on us. He has not given us the ability to do **everything!** But at the same time, we should agree with God regarding who He says we are and concerning what He says He will do. We should have confidence that whatever God calls us to do He will also enable us to do!

When we do not agree with God concerning His call on our lives and do not trust Him to enable us to be successfully obedient to that call, God calls our disagreement "unbelief," and unbelief is a sin. The effect of unbelief is seen throughout the history of the Church . . . For example, many are caught up on the performance merry-go-round. They believe they must meet certain standards of performance in order to feel good about themselves. We also tend to set standards for others as well. In both cases, we are setting ourselves up for failure and disappointment. Then, on the other hand, you may be unusually talented and experiencing great success at the performance game. If this be the case, I would caution you to not mistake pride for positive self-worth. God insists that we look to Him for our enablement. If you are looking to yourself for security and value, there will eventually be some failure or some form of discipline to turn you toward Him. He desires to be first place in your life and He desires to partner with you in every area of endeavor.

God does have a solution for this problem. God's solution for every behavioral problem is wrapped up in what Christ did for us at Calvary. When I think about Christ hanging on the cross, I think about how God placed upon Him all my sins, both past and future. Then the Bible tells us that the wrath of

God was poured out on Him so that Jesus cried out, "Father, why have you forsaken me?" When Jesus finally said, "It is finished," He was literally saying IT IS PAID IN FULL. The words were words you would see written at the bottom of a bill that no longer had a balance.

So your sins were actually paid for in full thousands of years ago, long before you were even born! When you accept Christ as your Savior, you are accepting that what He accomplished on the cross was to pay for every sin you would commit for your entire life! How many sins did the Father punish? He punished all of them as He poured out His wrath on His Son Jesus that day.

I think many women in the church think that some sins are worse than others. Some sins, they believe, carry a heavier penalty. Some women think that they are going to heaven but they do not believe God is pleased with them. Do you think God's holiness is less grieved by some sins and more grieved by others? It is true that, as our Father, sins are more grievous to Him that affect people in a greater way, i.e. adultery affects many people; murder can affect many people, etc. The Bible tells us, however, that as far as His holiness is concerned, to be guilty of one violation of the law is to be guilty of the whole law. He is grieved by **all** sin! But no matter what the severity of our sin, the blood of Jesus has washed away the penalty of all sin equally. Let's choose to agree with what the Bible says!

Is it possible for a person to sin more than God will forgive? Can a person fill up or overflow God's capacity to forgive and redeem? If you are a child of God, the only way God would pour out His wrath on you is if He chose to ignore the wrath He poured out on Christ at Calvary! He would not DISHONOR Christ like that! He would not dismiss the value of what Christ did on the cross!

"God made him who had no sin to be sin for us, so that in him we might become the righteousness of God" (2 Corinthians 5:21).

When you accepted Jesus' gift, God imputed the righteousness that belonged to Christ to you.

It is yours. You cannot do anything to become any *less* righteous or any *more* righteous because your righteousness is *His* righteousness! He assigned it to you.

Sin does affect us and is destructive to us. Therefore there are times when God has to discipline us just as we do our children. But it is key that you understand that when we act sinfully we are acting below what God by His grace has called and enabled us to do . . I ask you, if a man suddenly loses his mind, gets down on all fours and begins barking like a dog, is the man really a dog? Of course not; he is still a man despite what he thinks about himself! For those who are born again in Christ, sometimes we act out our lives in deception, like that man who thought he was a dog. We think we are worthless and unable to experience victory. We don't realize that we have been recreated by the hand of God. We underestimate our value. But our wrong thinking does not change the fact that God values us greatly! We have value in God's eyes no matter what we think, but we don't experience much of the good consequence of belonging to God when we are stuck in unbelief. Understanding the difference between our **actions** and our **value** enables us to reject our performance without devaluing ourselves.

With this kind of wrong thinking, we will never know who we really are. And if you do not know who you are, how can you mature in Christ? How many Christians have been walking with the Lord for their entire life but have made little progress in being transformed into His likeness? Very often, a lack of understanding about the total effectiveness of the cross of Jesus is at the root of their powerlessness to lead successful Christian lives. To become a genuinely satisfied woman who walks into the fullness of her destiny, you must agree with God in terms of what He says **Christ did for you, how valuable you are** and **who He has made you to be**!

Another major hindrance to our maturing in Christ is our *need for approval.* Sin created a separation between God and man. Jesus, through the cross, reconciled man to God. As a result, we have God's acceptance and approval and do not need man's approval. This is called the doctrine of reconciliation.

Many women blame & punish others as well as themselves when things do not go well or when they don't feel good about themselves. In reality, Christ's substitution death on the cross paid the penalty for our sin, and he gave us His righteousness as a bonus. As I mentioned in a previous chapter, whom can we blame or hold accountable for sins when Jesus has redeemed us? How can I blame someone else when Jesus has redeemed her life? When I do this, I am setting myself up as a higher judge above Christ and His authority and ability to judge! This is one of the many deceptions the enemy has embedded in the human belief system used to kill, steal and destroy individuals and the church. And this is a sin against God.

Shame arises out of a negative evaluation of our past performance or a critical opinion of our physical appearance. The result of shame is a sense of worthlessness and hopelessness. God's answer to this problem is *regeneration*. When you are regenerated, a new "you" is created by the Holy Spirit. There is nothing negative about the new you. In fact, you are made perfect through regeneration. Because of your faith in Christ, He has made you into a new person. God created this new person from nothing. You have a brand-new nature with new potential and new capacities. *We must come into agreement with God about these things!*

Romans 6:1-11 teaches us that we died with Christ and have been resurrected with Him unto new life. Sin no longer has **spiritual** or **legal** power over us. *"For we know that our old self was crucified with him so that the body of sin might be done away with, that we should no longer be slaves to sin—"* (Romans 6:6). The commentary of The New Spirit Filled Life Bible explains, "The body of sin refers to the sinful nature within us, not to the human body. The Greek verb translated done away with does not mean to become extinct, but to be defeated or deprived of power."[30] In other words, Christ has defeated the power sin once had over the body. As believers, although struggles with sin in the flesh still occur, they no longer have power over us. Christians "have died to the love of sin and the ruling power of sin."[31] However, we are not yet dead to all of it's influences. It is up to us to daily crucify the flesh and not allow sin to reign in our bodies. Your new spiritual self (the redeemed one) resides in your body right along with your old soul self (the unrighteous one). They are at war with one another. In order to bring the *old you* into line with the *new you*, Roman 12:2 tells us to "...be transformed by the renewing of your mind." In other words, study the Word of God, meditate on it and begin to put it in action in your life. Your mind, will and emotions will begin to come into agreement with God and with the new you.

If you struggle with the areas mentioned here, I suggest you do an in-depth study on the above doctrines and come into agreement with God concerning them. As you align your old nature found in your mind, will and emotions with the Word of God, you will experience peace, satisfaction and abundant living.

Significance and worth are found only in Christ Jesus! There is no greater worth than to be so valuable that the One who is more valuable than all that is would die for you. Do you see this? You were paid for with that which has more worth than anything that exists, the life of the Son of God, and *that fact makes your worth equal to his.* He determined your life to be worth His life! As you align your thoughts with God's thoughts about you, you will develop a new kind of self esteem. We call it God esteem.

God has declared you righteous and your worth is that of a child of God and a royal priest of God. You were chosen by God because He loved you. Why run to other people in search of significance? He has said you are of supreme worth! He has also given you the most valuable purpose for your life! Accept all the things in your life you cannot change. Accept how God has fashioned you and who He made you to be. Accept the gifts and talents God has given you. Accept who you are in Christ Jesus!

If you want to come into the fullness of the destiny God has planned for you, you must break the habit of using possessions, people, performance, and the judgments from others or yourself as your standard of evaluation. Begin using *God's truth* for your standard. Proverbs 23:7 says, "For as a man thinks, so he is." Memorize and meditate on who *God says you are*. Get into agreement with God and your thought life will begin to change. And watch out for your tongue. The words you speak about yourself should be the same words God speaks concerning you. Daily tell yourself and your Christian friends who you are in Christ!

The more truth you have in your mind, the easier it is for you to discern the lies of the one that comes to steal, kill, and destroy. The affirmation of God's love and acceptance will help you to come into agreement with God. You will begin to receive a new self image and you will have taken another step on your journey to become a Satisfied Woman!

ROAD STOP:

Do you recognize the lies of the enemy that are embedded in your belief system? Any thought *contrary* to God's Word concerning you is a lie. Ask the Holy Spirit to help you identify the lies that trouble you. Then find God's answer – His Truth that breaks the power of the lie. Memorize these Truths and when the lies try to enter your mind, speak the truth against them and do not allow yourself to take hold of the lie – don't allow them in. *Guard your mind* with the Truth found in Scripture concerning *who you are* as a *new creation in Christ*!

CHAPTER TWENTY-TWO

A Gratifying, Satisfying Abundant Life!

"the thief comes only to steal and kill and destroy;
I have come that they may have life,
and have it to the full" (John 10:10)

"But godliness with contentment is great gain"
(1 Timothy 6:6)

According to 1 Timothy 6:6, contentment, when added to godliness, brings us great gain or abundance. The Amplified Bible states it like this, *"(And it is, indeed, a source of immense profit, for) godliness accompanied with contentment (that contentment which is a sense of inward sufficiency) is great and abundant gain."* Because you are reading this book, I know you desire the abundance in life that Christ has promised in John 10:10, *"the thief comes only to steal and kill and destroy; I have come that they may have life, and have it to the full."* As you make **a decision to aim** for abundance, the power of Christ that resides inside of you will energize you to persevere to the achievement of that goal. Achieving the abundant life which is gratifying and satisfying comes through the process of allowing God's Word to change *the way you think*, *the way you feel*, and *the things you value* until you are truly walking in genuine supernatural satisfaction!

We have journeyed in the Book of Ecclesiastes where King Solomon, the son of King David and a very wise King, wrote about three stages of life: birth, death, and the stage between birth and death. In the first two stages, we enter and leave life with nothing. In order to walk out the journey between birth and death, however, we can conclude that we need some things such as food, clothing and shelter in order to survive. As we continue on our journey, we discover that as long as these three needs of food, clothing and shelter are met, we can experience true contentment, but we must avoid the traps. Our enemy who desires to steal, kill and destroy (John 10:10) has set traps designed to ensnare us that he may grab hold of our joy and cause us to be less than satisfied with what God has given us.

We have learned that people, power, position, promotion, popularity nor wealth will lead us to genuine satisfaction. Although there is nothing wrong with having money in itself, the Bible does warn us in Matthew 19:24, *"Again I tell you, it is easier for a camel to go through the eye of a needle than for a rich man to enter the kingdom of God."* Having a lot of money can give a certain kind of freedom and can allow a woman to do just about anything she wants but it also comes with its own set of temptations of which she must guard herself. A rich woman may experience greater temptations to live selfishly and to manipulate and dominate people with her money. Although the rich may be prone to serving mammon before God – exalting wealth, position and power above Him in their lives, the poor are susceptible to fall in this area as well. If the poor man is envious of the rich and focused on obtaining things instead of focusing on and trusting God, then he has fallen into a different kind of trap set with the same kind of bait –that bait being **the lust for things.**

If God's purpose for you is to *receive material blessings, recognize* that it is God *Himself* Who has blessed you with wealth and guard yourself from worshipping mammon and what it brings to your life. The thing is to keep **first things first** and **the first thing is God**! One discipline that helps all of us to place God above riches is to honor Him with a minimum of a tenth of our earnings. Obedience or not to this spiritual discipline, tells where our hearts lie – with God or with mammon. When we tithe we are saying that we realize that God has given to us all that we have and that without His grace, we would have nothing.

It is important to be content wherever God has you, whether rich or poor, counting the blessings He has for you *where* He has you. Ask God to give you an attitude as the Apostle Paul had, "*...Actually, I don't have a sense of needing anything personally.*

I've learned by now to be quite content whatever my circumstances. I'm just as happy with little as with much, with much as with little. I've found the recipe for being happy whether full or hungry, hands full or hands empty. Whatever I have, wherever I am, I can make it through anything in the One who makes me who I am..." (Philippians 4:10-14 MSG). Live according to Matthew 6:33, "But more than anything else, put God's work first and do what he wants. Then the other things will be yours as well" (CEV). God asks that we seek Him, the things of His Kingdom and His righteousness. When we keep first things first, then He Himself may choose to bless us with wealth. This is different than the foolishness and even hurtfulness of seeking after things and possessions – the person who does so, risks being utterly destroyed in both body and soul for eternity. Phil 3:18-19, *"for as I have often told you before and now say again even with tears, many live as enemies of the cross of Christ. Their destiny is destruction, their god is their stomach, and their glory is in their shame. Their mind is on earthly things."* This verse is the crux of the whole matter. If my heart and mind are focused on things, if I am lusting after possessions instead of running after God, then I have made possessions an idol in my life. If you find yourself at this place, you should repent and turn your focus back to Jesus.

Along our journey to satisfaction we will need to cultivate the mind of Christ – making His mind, our mind. This is how we prevent Satan from successfully ensnaring us and robbing us of joy and satisfaction. A satisfied woman needs to have a *(1) yielded, (2) servant, (3) one-purpose, (4)shielded and (5)vigilant* mind in order to **hold** onto satisfaction.

Circumstances do not ensnare a satisfied woman, causing her to lose her satisfaction, because she has a *yielded mind.* Her mind is yielded to the plan of God for her life. She understands that God is ultimately in control. Therefore, whatever situation she finds herself in, she knows God is using it to work it into His eternal plan for her life according to His purpose for her life.

Satan cannot use *people* and their attitudes or actions towards a satisfied woman to rob her of her satisfaction. She has the mind of a <u>servant</u> that looks to the concerns of others rather than her own. She refrains from putting her expectations on others. This frees her to accept others where they are on their spiritual journey. She realizes that they, like her, are God's concern and His workmanship. *"for we are God's workmanship, created in Christ Jesus to do good works, which God prepared in advance for us to do." (Ephesians 2:10).*

The enemy cannot use *material things* to rob a satisfied woman of her satisfaction because she has a <u>one purpose mind</u>. She is focused on Christ Jesus and Him alone and the riches of His glory that await her. She is concerned about things only to the degree that they can help her grow in her likeness to Jesus. She does not need a lot of possessions because her life is surrendered to God and she knows He will take care of her. Worry and anxiety are things of the past.

The enemy cannot use the *temptation of worry* as bait to ensnare a satisfied woman in order to steal her satisfaction. She has a <u>vigilant and shielded mind</u>. Her daily thoughts are guarded by the *peace of God.*

As she communes with the Lord, casting her cares upon Him, anxiety in any form becomes unacceptable. She knows that worry and anxiety are symptoms of not trusting God and she knows that God is totally trustworthy and faithful. As she focuses on Him, God keeps her mind at peace to focus on pursuing His Kingdom and His righteousness. As she takes care of His business and stays focused on and trusts in Him, He takes care of her business... *"but seek first his kingdom and his righteousness, and all these things will be given to you as well." (Matthew 6:33).*

To thoroughly study the subject of satisfaction one can read the book of Ecclesiastes in the Holy Bible. King Solomon after reviewing in Chapter 2 four negative arguments concerning life and it's purpose concludes that life really **is** worth living! Warren W. Wiersbe shares in his book "Be Satisfied" that Solomon tells us to trust God, do our work, accept what God sends us, and enjoy each day of our lives to the glory of God (Ecclesiastes 3:12-15, 22: 5:18-20; 8:15; 9:7-10).[31]

We can conclude from Ecclesiastes that if we are to be satisfied, we need to live life as:

1. a VENTURE – do not be overly cautious – explore it by faith (11:1-6)
2. a PRESENT – enjoy it knowing God is good Creator & righteous Judge (11:7-12:8)
3. a UNIVERSITY – learn lessons, recognize human limitations and gain a godly vision for life (12:9-12)
4. a STEWARDSHIP – fear God – submit to His commands in reverence (12:13-14)

Remember, if you have a physical craving and the need for food, shelter and clothing has been met, then that craving is an unhealthy desire that could develop into a lust that will **control** your life. That hollow hole was placed in your soul by God and it can only be satisfied by filling it with Him. If you try to fill it with material things, people, men, education, recognition, promotion, etc. or drugs and alcohol, the satisfaction will be temporary because those things are only imitations. As you seek the imitation, the craving will return again and again at a heightened level. When these needs are met and you still feel empty, you need to recognize that it is not a physical or material craving. It is a craving that comes from *your spiritual needs not being met*. This physical craving is a symptom of a spiritual hunger for His Presence. God has placed that void there and He wants to fill it if you will only let Him. In Heart Cry Magazine, Issue 26 of 2003, Jonathan Edwards put it this way,

> *"the enjoyment of God is the only happiness with which our souls can be satisfied.* Fathers and mothers, husbands, wives, or children, or the company of earthly friends are but shadows, but enjoyment of God is the substance. These are but scattered beams, but God is the sun. These are but streams, but God is the fountain. These are but drops, but God is the ocean."

When you live through faith in Jesus Christ, a sense of blessing accompanies you everywhere you go, and life is worth living. You can be satisfied no matter what God allows in your life. Having this God-ward attitude and doing that which is pleasing to Him, out of reverence for Him, is the only thing that can bring satisfaction to your soul. When we refuse the lies and all that exalts itself against the knowledge of God and we begin walking in the truth of the light of what God has told us to be true, then we experience the abundance of God within our innermost being and soul. We have no need. We are completely complete and fulfilled. We live life with a sense of lacking nothing. The secret that so very few people have learned is that **satisfaction is obtainable**, but there is only one route that leads to it. That route is the road of godliness. **Devotion to God** is required to navigate the road of godliness; devotion that demands expression in a way of life *that reflects the character of God*. It is a road in which you will need to *seek God* and *seek to express your devotion to Him through your manner of living*. It is a road where you will want to develop a *secure* and *submitted* mind. Submission to the will of God for your life will keep you on the road of godliness. It is a road of *choosing* to think God's thoughts as revealed in the Bible, to *obey* God's commands: *accept* God's answers about Himself and about how you are to treat others; *to believe, accept and act on* what God says *about who you are* and what you are to do with your life, about your circumstances, and about what choices you make.

The road of godliness will lead you to genuine, lasting satisfaction and to the overflowing, abundant life that Jesus promised us. Remember though that you are on a journey – traveling the road of godliness *on your way to* the satisfied life overflowing with abundance. You won't get to your goal in an instant. This is a process so don't despair when you don't get there overnight. Give yourself permission to stumble. God has given you that permission and He has made provision for you should you do so. The journey has been mapped out for you. When you fall because of sin, confess your sin for what it is – sin. He will forgive you and cleanse you of all unrighteousness (1 John 1:9). He just asks that you *begin*

– start walking. You are not alone on the journey. While walking out the journey, you will experience contentment in knowing you are with God and He Himself will perfect everything which concerns you according to His Word, *"the Lord will perfect that which concerns me; Your mercy and loving-kindness, O Lord, endure forever – forsake not the works of Your own hands" (Psalm 138:8 AMP)*. Yes, life is worth living and you can be a satisfied woman! It is a wonderful thing and as a satisfied woman, it is available to experience an abundant life – one that is gratifying and satisfying; overflowing (or abounding) with sufficiency and contentment. However, we have seen that personal satisfaction does not come easily and it does not come naturally. First, you must be alive through faith in Jesus Christ. Then no matter what, you can be satisfied!

Recognize God's love, grace and mercy along the way to the abundant life promised to you *whose behavior reflects devotion to God* and who *are satisfied living your life for Him*. As you walk into the abundant life God has for you, your heart will overflow with thanksgiving and rejoicing. And the fullness of the destiny God so lovingly planned for you will begin to unfold before you.

Now it is up to you to begin your journey. Let each step be filled with faith. Walk with an *expectation* to become a genuinely satisfied woman! Remember, most things that are worthwhile do not come easy. Remember satisfaction is learned and yet it is a spiritual condition. Godliness and satisfaction were not instantaneous with salvation but require effort. The satisfied life can not happen without deliberate, intentional effort. It will only occur if you are willing to go to a deeper level with God and if you have a willingness to cooperate with Him. The more effort and time you give to seeking godliness with contentment, the closer you will be to experiencing the fullness of your destiny! – ***Worth, peace, fulfillment, and abundance – is the destiny of the woman who pursues God and is content knowing and accepting that He alone rules! This is a Satisfied Woman!***

Perhaps our paths will cross along the journey. I hope they do. If not, I look forward to seeing you at the finish line!

"brothers, I do not consider myself yet to have taken hold of it. But one thing I do: Forgetting what is behind and straining toward what is ahead, I press on toward the goal to win the prize for which God has called me heavenward in Christ Jesus. All of us who are mature should take such a view of things. And if on some point you think differently, that too God will make clear to you" (Phil 3:13-15).

Appendix A

L et's begin our journey by taking an honest look into ourselves to see where we currently are living in terms of living satisfied and fulfilled lives.

<u>Satisfaction Quesionnaire</u>

Be honest with yourself and write out or circle the answer(s) that best describe where you are currently living at this time:

(1) I find myself complaining...

Rarely (if Ever); Sometimes; Monthly; Weekly; Daily; Constantly

(2) I am discontent when I think about my:

Work; Home life; Marriage; Parenting; Social life; Financial life

Who God Has Made Me to Be; My Family of Origin; My gifts and/or talents

Past Choices; Past Circumstances; Present Circumstances; Future Other _____

(3) Answer the question why you think you are discontent with each area you have circled above. Use another sheet of paper if needed.

(4) Where do you go or what do you do to bring yourself a sense of fulfillment and satisfaction?

_____

_____

_____

_____

_____

_____

5) Why do you think your above answer leads you to a sense of satisfaction? _____

_____

_____

_____

_____

(6) Does this sense of fulfillment & satisfaction last long? _____

How long? _____

_____

(7) If you could name three things that you could change that would bring fulfillment and satisfaction to your life, what would they be in order of perceived value? _____

_____

_____

_____

_____

(8) Why do you think that to be so? _____

_____

_____

_____

_____

_____

_____

And, how often do you think about this? _____

_____

_____

_____

(9) Give your definition of what it means to be a satisfied woman: _____

_____

_____

_____

_____

_____

(10) What part do you think you play in having a satisfied life? _____

_____

_____

_____

(11) Do you believe the Bible is the inspired Word of God and teaches Christians how to live life to its fullest? Yes or No

(12) How much time per week do you currently spend in prayer? _____ and/or the bible? _____

_____

_____

_____

_____

(13) Have you received Jesus Christ as both Lord & Savior? Yes or No

Do you know the difference? Yes or No

(14) What wisdom do you have for yourself in how you might be able to seek after and increase the level of satisfaction you experience in your life?

_____

_____

_____

Record below any other thoughts that have come to your mind concerning your satisfaction at this time:

_____

_____

_____

Today's Date: _____

Now put on your walking shoes, turn back to chapter one and let's begin the journey into God's Word. Here you will find the Answer to your life's quest for genuine satisfaction.

Once you have completed the book and after you begin to put into practice the principles found herein, you may want to retake this questionnaire.

APPENDIX B

REMINDERS FOR THE JOURNEY

✍

On Your Journey to Discover **True Worth, Peace, Fulfillment & Abundance,** you will be cultivating contentment and growing in satisfaction daily. However, this is a life-long journey. As you walk out these principles, your level of satisfaction will increase accordingly. *You may want to keep the following steps in a place where they will serve as a DAILY reminder to you. The acrostic below may help you.. The following steps begin with the letters that when put together spell out our goal which is to be*

S A T I S F I E D

In Him!

STEP

1. **S** eek God. Seek first the Kingdom of God and His righteousness. Seek to know Him more through *His Word* and *prayer.* *"Then you will call upon me and come and pray to me, and I will listen to you. You will seek me and find me when you seek me with all your heart"* (*Jeremiah 29:12-13*).

2. **A** ccept **God for who He is**! A sovereign God Who loves you with an everlasting love. An all- powerful, all- knowing, omnipresent (always with you), unchanging God who will never leave you.

3. **T** ransform –Be transformed as you renew your mind about yourself according to what God says— not according to performance, other's opinions, your past, etc. God is not deceived. He really knows who you are so *throw off the lies* and be transformed as you *accept* His Truth! (Acceptance is a process that *begins* with a *decision* but continues until it *develops into sincere feelings* of the heart. At this point, deci-

sion begins to be seen in your *daily choices and actions*.) **Be transformed as you**

(a) accept **that you are significant to Him**. You must by an act of your own will, choose to believe that you are what God says that you are. Reject thoughts that tell you that you are less than what God tells you. "*But you are a chosen people, a royal priesthood, a holy nation, a people belonging to God, that you may declare the praises of him who called you out of darkness into his wonderful light*" (*1 Peter 2:9*).

(*b*) accept **that God did a good job when He made you** – it was God who put you in your birth family, that it was God who made you the person you are in terms of family origin, gifts, talents and personality.

(*c*) accept **the life He has given you at every turn and in every season – no matter what!** "*For I know the plans I have for you,*" declares the LORD, "*plans to prosper you and not to harm you, plans to give you* *hope and a future"* (Jeremiah 29:11). *"And we know that in all things God works for the good of those who love him, who have been called according to his purpose"* (Romans 8:28). Believe God's promises to you and that they will work in your life just as they did the Apostle Paul's.

4. <u>**I** ntentionally cultivate the mind of Christ</u> – a *yielded, servant, one-purpose, vigilant, shielded* mind in order that you may discern and avoid the enemy's snares on the journey that are designed steal, kill and destroy your life, joy and satisfaction.

5. <u>**S** ubmit to *God's sovereignty*</u> in your life and to the ***Holy Spirit's power and leading***, allowing Him to reproduce within you His godly character. (See the Beatitudes found in Matthew Chapter 5). The fruit of His spirit will burst forth as found in Galatians 5:22-23: (love, joy, peace, patience, kindness, goodness, faithfulness, gentleness and self-control).

6. **F** orgive **others** and **yourself**; receive God's forgiveness; and give forgiveness. When you stumble, confess your sin, receive God's forgiveness and cleansing. *"If we confess our sins, he is faithful and just and will forgive us our sins and purify us from all unrighteousness" (1 John 1:9).*

7. **I** dentify your beliefs through your emotions; reject those that do not line up with God's Word (the lies) and replace them with God's truth.

8. **E** xpect spiritual warfare but **Expect victory** in it! The enemy of God does not want you to be free to walk in the abundance God has for you as a satis-fied woman! But remember, "the one who is in you is greater than the one who is in the world" (1 John 4:4). Call upon the Lord for His help! "You can do everything through Him who gives you strength" (Philippians 4:13) and "…Overwhelming victory is yours through Christ who loves you" (Romans 8:37 NLV).

9. **D** on't quit! No matter what, don't quit! Continue moving forward. Begin each day as a new day! Don't look to the past. Stay focused on Christ and the riches of His glory. Press on toward the prize. *"Brothers, I do not consider myself yet to have taken hold of it. But one thing I do: Forgetting what is behind and straining toward what is ahead, I press on toward the goal to win the prize for which God has called me heavenward in Christ Jesus. All of us who are mature should take such a view of things. And if on some point you think differently, that too God will make clear to you"* (Phil 3:13-15).

Worth, peace, fulfillment, and abundance –
is the destiny of the woman who pursues God and is
content knowing and accepting that
He alone rules!

She is a

SATISFIED WOMAN!

WHAT ECCLESIASTES HAS TO SAY ABOUT *LIFE*

❦

As you walk out your journey to satisfaction, remember the wisdom found in the Book of Ecclesiastes summed up with VPUS as shown below:

I. **Life is a VENTURE – do not be overly cautious – explore it by faith (Ecclesiastes 11:1-6)**

1 Cast your bread upon the waters,

for after many days you will find it again.

2 Give portions to seven, yes to eight,

> for you do not know what disaster may
>
> come upon the land.

3 If clouds are full of water,

> they pour rain upon the earth.
>
> Whether a tree falls to the south
>
> or to the north,
>
> in the place where it falls, there will it lie.

4 Whoever watches the wind will not plant;

> whoever looks at the clouds will not reap.

5 As you do not know the path of the wind,

> or how the body is formed [a] in
>
> a mother's womb,
>
> so you cannot understand the work of God,
>
> the Maker of all things.

6 Sow your seed in the morning,

> and at evening let not your hands be idle,
>
> for you do not know which will succeed,
>
> whether this or that,
>
> or whether both will do equally well.

II. Life is a PRESENT – enjoy it knowing God is a good Creator & a righteous Judge (Ecclesiastes 11:7-12:8)

7 Light is sweet,

and it pleases the eyes to see the sun.

8 However many years a man may live,

let him enjoy them all.

But let him remember the days of darkness,

for they will be many.

Everything to come is meaningless.

9 Be happy, young man, while you are young,

and let your heart give you joy in the days of

your youth.

Follow the ways of your heart

and whatever your eyes see,

but know that for all these things

God will bring you to judgment.

10 So then, banish anxiety from your heart

and cast off the troubles of your body,

for youth and vigor are meaningless.

Ecclesiastes 12

1 Remember your Creator

in the days of your youth,

before the days of trouble come

and the years approach when you will say,

"I find no pleasure in them"-

2 before the sun and the light

and the moon and the stars grow dark,

and the clouds return after the rain;

3 when the keepers of the house tremble,

and the strong men stoop,

when the grinders cease because they are
few,

and those looking through the windows
grow dim;

4 when the doors to the street are closed

and the sound of grinding fades;

when men rise up at the sound of birds,

but all their songs grow faint;

5 when men are afraid of heights

and of dangers in the streets;

when the almond tree blossoms

and the grasshopper drags himself along

and desire no longer is stirred.

Then man goes to his eternal home

and mourners go about the streets.

6 Remember him—before the silver cord is severed,

or the golden bowl is broken;

before the pitcher is shattered at the spring,

or the wheel broken at the well,

7 and the dust returns to the ground it came from,

and the spirit returns to God who gave it.

8 "Meaningless! Meaningless!" says the Teacher. [a]

"Everything is meaningless!"

III. Life is a UNIVERSITY – learn lessons, recognize human limitations and gain a godly vision for life (Ecclesiastes 12:9-12)

9 Not only was the Teacher wise, but also he imparted knowledge to the people.

He pondered and searched out and set in
order many proverbs.

10 The Teacher searched to find just the right
words, and what he wrote was upright and
true.

11 The words of the wise are like goads,
their collected sayings like firmly
embedded nails — given by one Shepherd.

12 Be warned, my son, of anything in addition
to them.
Of making many books there is no end, and
much study wearies the body.

IV. Life is a STEWARDSHIP – fear God – submit to His commands in reverence (Ecclesiastes 12:13-14)

13 Now all has been heard;
here is the conclusion of the matter:
Fear God and keep his commandments,
for this is the whole duty of man.

14 For God will bring every deed into judgment,

including every hidden thing,

whether it is good or evil.

APPENDIX D

Scriptural Confessions for a Healthy Belief System

"The righteousness based on faith speaks...The Word is near you, in your mouth and in your heart' — that is the Word of faith which we are preaching...for with the heart a person believes, resulting in righteousness, and with the mouth he confesses, resulting in salvation ." **Romans 10:6-10**

I AM a new creation - a new person altogether in Christ Jesus. Old things have passed away; all things have become fresh and new! **II Corinthians 5:17**

I AM already cleansed because of the Word Jesus has spoke to me. **John 15:9**

I HAVE BEEN made the righteousness of God. I am completely justified by faith apart from the works of the law, therefore, I have peace with God today and can stand in His presence without guilt, shame or a sense of inferiority. **Romans 5:1, II Corinthians 5:21**

Jesus has RECONCILED ME by His death and presents me to the Father unblameable, unaccusable and without reproach, since I continue in faith firmly established and steadfast, not moved away from the truth of God's Word that I have heard. **Colossians 1:22-23**

The Father HAS QUALIFIED ME to share in this inheritance and has drawn me to Himself out of the control and dominion of darkness and has transferred me in to the kingdom of the Son of His love. **Colossians 1:12-13**

Since I HAVE BEEN RAISED WITH CHRIST to a **new** life, I aim at and seek the rich eternal treasures that are above, where Christ is seated at the right hand of God. I set my mind and keep it set on what is above, not on the things that are on the earth. For as far as this world is concerned, I have died and my new real life is hidden with Christ in God. **I Corinthians 1:30**

Therefore, I have considered the members of my body dead to immorality, impurity, passion, evil desire and greed. I put away and rid myself of anger, rage, bad feelings toward others, curses and slander and abusive speech from my mouth. **Colossians 3:5, 8**

I let my speech at all times be gracious, pleasant and winsome, seasoned with salt, so that I may never be at a loss to know how I ought to answer anyone who puts a question to me. I clothe myself, as God's chosen one, purified, holy and well loved by God Himself by putting on behavior marked by tender hearted pity and mercy, kind feelings, a lowly opinion of myself, gentle ways and patience which is tireless and long suffering, and has the power to endure whatever comes, with good temper. **Colossians 3:12**

I let all men know and perceive and recognize my unselfishness, my considerateness, and my forbearing spirit. **Philippians 4:5**

I look carefully how I walk. I live purposefully and worthily and accurately, not as the unwise and witless, but as a wise sensible, intelligent person, making the very most of the time, buying up each opportunity because the days are evil. Therefore, I am not vague, thoughtless, and foolish but I understand and firmly grasp what the will of the Lord is. **Ephesians 5:15-16**

I have strength for all things in Christ Who empowers me. I am ready for anything and equal to anything through Him who infuses inner strength into me; I am self sufficient in Christ's sufficiency. **Philippians 4:13**

I will establish myself in righteousness and I will be far from even the thought of oppression or destruction for I shall not fear, and far from terror for it shall not come near me. **Isaiah 54:14**

I listen to God's Word, therefore, I live securely and I'm at ease from the dread of evil. **Proverbs 1:33**

I thank You, Lord, that my love abounds still more and more in knowledge and all discernment, that I approve the things that are excellent and that I am sincere and without offense until the day of Christ. **Philippians 1:9**

I am a child of God by faith in Christ Jesus. **Galatians 3:26**

If the Lord delights in a man's way, he makes his steps firm. **Psalm 37:23**

Commit to the Lord whatever you do, and your plans will succeed. **Proverbs 16:3**

It is because of him that you are in Christ Jesus, who has become for us wisdom from God—that is, our righteousness, holiness and redemption. **1 Corinthians 1:30**

He guides the humble in what is right and teaches them his way. **Psalm 25:9**

If we confess our sins, he is faithful and just and will forgive us our sins and purify us from all unrighteousness. **I John 1:9**

I am established in righteousness. I am far from oppression in my mind; and fear and terror will not come near me to control me. No weapon formed against me shall prosper and every tongue that accuses me in judgment shall be shown to be in the wrong. **Isaiah 54:14, 17**

I let the peace of God rule in my heart and mind and I am thankful to God in all things. **Colossians 3:15**

Father, I thank You that the peace of God, which surpasses all knowledge, is guarding my heart and mind in Christ Jesus. I command my mind to dwell only on that which is true, honorable, pure, lovely excellent and worthy of praise. **Philippians 4:7-8**

ENDNOTES

⌒

[1] Blue Letter Bible. "Dictionary and Word Search for 'perissos' (Strong's 4053)'". Blue Letter Bible. 1996-2002. 27 Jul 2006. http://www.blueletterbible.org.

[2] Warren Wiersbe, *Be Satisfied* (Colorado Springs, CO, Cook Communications 2005), 11.

[3] Warren Wiersbe, *Be Satisfied* (Colorado Springs, CO, Cook Communications 2005), 19.

[4] The American Heritage® Dictionary of the English Language, Fourth Edition Copyright © 2000 by Houghton Mifflin Company. Published by Houghton Mifflin Company. All rights reserved.

[5] Holman Bible Publishers (Nashville, TN web: www. broadmanholman.com). © Copyright 1991 Holman Bible Publishers. All rights reserved. International copyright secured.

[6] With thanks to Michael Fletcher, whose sermon inspired these thoughts.

[7] *New Spirit- Filled Life Bible*, Copyright ©2002 by Thomas Nelson, Inc. All rights reserved, 792.

[8] Carnegie, *How To Stop Worrying and Start Living* (New York: Simon and Schuster, 1948), 19 & 96.

[9] William J. Bouwsma, John Calvin, *A Sixteenth-Century Portrait* (New York: Oxford University Press, 1988), 37.

[10] Robert J. Morgan, *Nelson's Complete Book of Stories, Illustrations, & Quotes* (Nashville, TN: 2003), Copyright © by Robert J. Morgan. All rights reserved, 801.

[11]Robert J. Morgan, *Nelson's Complete Book of Stories, Illustrations, & Quotes* (Nashville, TN: 2003), Copyright © by Robert J. Morgan. All rights reserved, 803-804.

[12]W. E. Vine, *Expository Dictionary of New Testament Words* (Grand Rapids, MI: Zondervan Publishing House:1952), 162.

[13]humble. Dictionary.com. *Dictionary.com Unabridged (v 1.0.1)*, Based on the Random House Unabridged Dictionary, © Random House, Inc. 2006. http://dictionary.reference.com/browse/humble (accessed: September 27, 2006).

[14]Robert J. Morgan, *Nelson's Complete Book of Stories, Illustrations, & Quotes* (Nashville, TN: 2003), Copyright © by Robert J. Morgan. All rights reserved, 456.

[15]Clyde S. Kilby, *Minority of One: A Biography of Jonathan Blanchard* (Grand Rapids, MI: Eerdmans Publishing House, 1959), 38.

[16] Pastor Jonathan Goebel sermon illustration 2005, Manna Church, Lumberton, NC.

[17]Patrick Kavanaugh, *The Spiritual Lives of Great Composers* (Nashville: Sparrow Press, 1992), 13.

[18]Pastor Jonathan Goebel sermon illustration 2005, Manna Church, Lumberton, NC.

[19]V. Raymond Edman, *The Disciplines of Life* (Minneapolis: World Wide Publications, 1948), 202.

[20]A.W. Tozer, *The Pursuit of God* (Camphill, PA: Christian Publications, Inc. 1993), 104.

[21]A.W. Tozer, *The Pursuit of God* (Camphill, PA: Christian Publications, Inc. 1993), 104.

[22]Pastor Dan Cormie at Sermon Central 2006, sermoncentral.com.

[23]Cited by Luis Palau, *"Experiencing God's Forgiveness"* Multnomah Press, 1984.

[24]Martin Luther, *Encyclopedia of Quotations* by R. Daniel Watkins (Peabody, Massachusetts: Hendrickson Pubishers 2001), 654.

[25]J. I. Packer, *Knowing God* (Downers Grove, IL: InterVarsity Press 1973), 23.

[26]Matthew Henry's Commentary, Marshall, Morgan & Scott,Ltd., copyright 1960 Copyright 1961 by Zondervan Publishing House, Grand Rapids, Michigan, (Matthew 27:26-32),1352.

[27]Ken Sande, *The Peace Maker* (Grand Rapids, MI: Baker Books 2006), 263.

[28]Elmer L. Towns, *My Father's Names* (Ventura, CA: Regal Books 1991). Names of God and descriptions were compiled from this book.

[29]Wayne Grudem, *Bible Doctrine: "Essential Teachings of the Christian Faith"* (Grand Rapids, MI: Zondervan 1999, 88.

[30]*New Spirit- Filled Life Bible*, Commentary on Romans 6:6, (Nashville, TN: Thomas Nelson, Inc. Copyright ©2002). All rights reserved, 1558.

[31]*New Spirit- Filled Life Bible*, Commentary on Romans 6:11, (Nashville, TN: Thomas Nelson, Inc. Copyright ©2002). All rights reserved, 1558.

[32]Warren Wiersbe, Be Satisfied (Colorado Springs, CO: Cook Communications 2005),123, 126.

Declaring His Answer
Ministries, Int'l.

❦

T he heart of **Declaring His Answer Ministries, Int'l** is to create hope and bring change to the lives of women. As a ministry of women to women in accordance with Titus 2:3-5 and 2 Cor 1:4, DHAM is a vehicle being used by the Holy Spirit to set women free and sanctify them with the Word of Truth. God's love and grace are enthusiastically proclaimed, and lies embedded in women's hearts are exposed as they discover their REAL identity found in Him. DHAM is also encouraging and leading women into a place of unity within the body of Christ and helping equip them for serving in their local churches.

Sarah is currently ministering through writing and speaking opportunities. Ministry efforts of

DHAM also include the Women's Center located in Lumberton, NC. In an effort to support pastors and Christian counselors, Declaring His Answer Women's Center offers support groups for REAL life challenges faced by women, i.e. divorce recovery, anger, sexual abuse, fear, low self worth, and post abortion trauma.

DHAM is an advocate for young women and their babies. They actively support crisis pregnancy center efforts through a project called "Sarah's Daughters' Bundle of Love." Project efforts help provide support and alternatives to abortion for teens and women who find themselves in a "crisis" pregnancy. Sarah's Daughters Project name was inspired by 1 Peter 3:6b *"You are her daughters if you do what is right and do not give way to fear" (NIV).*

DHAM operates by the laws governing "churches and organizations controlled by a church" as a not-for-profit ministry allowing contributors full tax advantages for their gifts.

Declaring His Answer Ministries' mission in a nutshell is to bring life to the lives of women by declaring to them the Word of the Lord, the Truth that will set them free and sanctify them; and to equip them to joyfully fulfill their destiny in God.

"Then you will know the truth, and the truth **will set you free**" *(John 8:32).*

"**Sanctify them** in the truth; Your word is truth" *John 17:17(NASB).*

Habbakuk **2:2**," *Then the LORD said to me, "Write my answer in large, clear letters on a tablet, so that a runner can read it and tell everyone else. (NLV)*

You may contact Declaring His Answer Ministries for consultation concerning organization for a ministry to women within your church.

We appreciate your prayers and/or love gift offering.

I WOULD LIKE TO HEAR FROM YOU!

If this book has helped you in your
understanding and search for satisfaction;
or if you feel you were led into a deeper relationship
with the Lord after reading this book, it would mean
so much to me to hear from you. I would be happy
to pray with you as you continue on your journey
from faith to faith and glory to glory to the
abundant life of a satisfied woman.
If you came into a relationship with the Lord as you
read the pages of this book, please inform me of
your decision to accept Christ's free gift of salvation
by emailing me at the address below with your
address and salvation date.
Praise to God our Father!
With love,
Sarah

You may CONTACT the author or SOW SEED into this ministry at:

Declaring His Answer Ministries, Inc.

404 W. 25th Street

Lumberton, NC 28358

Email: declaringhisanswer@nc.rr.com

Visit our web page at: www.declaringhisanswer.com

About the Author

∽∾∿

Sarah Goebel is a woman of faith who lives for and loves the Lord. Chosen by God to be a vessel of full time service to women, God has called her for His service to loose women from bondage to fear, low self esteem and lackadaisicalness and to help them walk into their destiny with God.

Sarah is Founder of Declaring His Answer Ministries, a woman to woman ministry that offers support groups for women's "real life" challenges, equips women for lay ministry opportunities, and more. Sarah has ministered in Romania along with her husband and has written several articles for a community paper before publishing her first book, Satisfied Woman.

Sarah is the mother of two children. Some have called Sarah a survivor, but she is more than that. She is a conqueror. She has experienced, and against all odds, reigned victorious through Christ over several life traumas and challenges including abandonment, physical challenges, betrayals, physical abuses and more. These triumphs enable her, with faith for their victory, to relate and minister to women who are in a season of affliction. (2 Cor 1:4 NASB), *"Blessed be....the Father of mercies and God of all comfort, Who comforts us in all our affliction so that we will be able to comfort those who are in any affliction with the comfort with which we ourselves are comforted by God."*

Sarah is currently on staff at Manna Church of Lumberton as Minister to Women and she also assists her husband with the church as the Senior Pastor's wife. She has been a student of the Word since 1983; has attended Covenant Love Family Christian College and is currently working on her degree of divinity at Grace College of Divinity in Fayetteville, NC.

You may contact the author for interviews & speaking engagements at:

Declaring His Answer Ministries, Int'l

404 W. 25th Street

Lumberton, NC 28358

or by email at DeclaringHisAnswer@nc.rr.com

Visit Sarah on the web at: www. DeclaringHisAnswer.com

Printed in the United States
65906LVS00001B/1-96

9 781600 348037